Getting Results the Agile Way

*A Personal Results System
for Work and Life*

J.D. Meier

For information, please contact us:

Address: Innovation Playhouse LLC
            PMB 325
            227 Bellevue Way NE
            Bellevue, WA 98004
Email: innovationplayhouse@gmail.com
Website: http://www.gettingresults.com

Agile Results® and Agile Way® are trademarks of Innovation Playhouse LLC in the United States and/or other countries.

Library of Congress Cataloging-in-Publication Data has been applied for.

ISBN: 978-0-9845482-0-0

Praise for
Getting Results the Agile Way

Agile Results delivers know-what, know-why and know-how for anyone who understands the value of momentum in making your moments count. In our rapidly changing world, J.D. Meier offers a comprehensive clarity to sort through the often confusing cloud of complexity and find the real opportunity in our lives.

Dr. Rick Kirschner
Bestselling author, speaker, trainer, coach, The Art of Change LLC

J.D. is the go-to-guy for getting results, and Agile Results demonstrates his distinct purpose – he shows how anyone can do anything, better. This book has simple, effective, powerful tools and ideas that are easy enough for everyone to apply in their work and lives, so that they get the results they'd like, even the impossible and the unexpected.

Janine de Nysschen
Changemaker and Purpose Strategist, Whytelligence

It's all too easy for me to put my head down and focus on tasks without considering the bigger picture of what I am working toward. Agile Results forces me to see the forest from the trees, to constantly change my perspective and view-scope so that I am not only working efficiently but also working effectively toward maximum results.

Jason Taylor
CTO, Security Innovation

Working in disaster response and developing countries usually puts me in complex and even vexing situations. It is easy to fall into a rut of doing tasks with no priority or losing track of the big picture, and in our small team, time is precious. Agile Results fits my work well — it reinforces natural practices that put outcomes and adaptation at the center of the day.

Eduardo Jezierski
VP of Engineering, InSTEDD

J.D.'s writing resonated with me. The Rule of 3 has provided clarity, teaching me to devote laser-like focus to my most important tasks. Combined with the Monday Vision and Friday Reflection, I've established the rhythm of results of which J.D. speaks. The price of success is now affordable, sustainable, and more satisfying. The simple, flexible, and now obvious imperatives of Agile Results are allowing me to seize my life back.

Jimmy May
Principal Performance Engineer, Microsoft

Have you ever wondered why sometimes you get amazing results and other times just can't seem to be effective? Have you ever dreamed about an "essence of productivity" that you could apply to life? J.D. has distilled the essence of productivity into simple and effective techniques that produce real results. It's really that simple.

Mark Curphey
Product Unit Manager, Microsoft

J.D. provides a comprehensive approach in not only handling the influx of information, but also has helped me to prioritize at a higher level. Being able to think of breaking the day, the week, and the month into manageable chunks has kept my sanity. He has not only helped me to prioritize daily work, but the bigger picture of life. While I have tried other organizational tricks and tips, J.D. Meier's methods have stuck with me and improved my work-life balance ... I have recommended him to all my co-workers and peers!

Chenelle Bremont
Microsoft X-Box team

To Eileen, Mom, Dad, Beck, and Brad

Acknowledgements

I'd like to thank the following people for help with this book:

Adam Grocholski, Alik Levin, Andrew Kazyrevich, Andy Eunson, Andrea Fox, Anutthara Bharadwaj, Brian Maslowski, Chaitanya Bijwe, Chenelle Bremont, Daniel Rubiolo Mendoza, David K. Stewart, David Wright, David Zinger, Dennis Groves, Don Willits, Donald Latumahina, Dr. Rick Kirschner, Eduardo Jezierski, Eileen Meier, Erin M. Karp, Ethan Zaghmut, Gloria Campbell, Gordon Meier, Janine de Nysschen, Jason Taylor, Jeremy Bostron, Jill Heron, Jimmy May, John Allen, John deVadoss, Julian Gonzalez, Juliet du Preez, Kevin Lam, Larry Brader, Loren Kohnfelder, Mark Curphey, Michael Kropp, Michael Stiefel, Mike de Libero, Mike Torres, Mohammad Al-Sabt, Molly Clark, Olivier Fontana, Patrick Lanfear, Paul Enfield, Per Vonge Nielsen, Peter Larsson, Phil Huang, Prashant Bansode, Praveen Rangarajan, Richard Diver, Rob Boucher Jr., Rohit Sharma, Rudolph Araujo, Samantha Sieverling, Sameer Tarey, Scott Hanselman, Scott Stabbert, Scott Young, Sean Platt, Srinath Vasireddy, Steve Kayser, Tom Draper, Vidya Vrat Agarwal, Wade Mascia

I would also like to thank my loyal readers of my blog, Sources of Insight (http://SourcesOfInsight.com), for their helpful feedback.

Contents at a Glance

Foreword

One thing is certain—change happens. It happens in your job and in your personal life. One of my favorite quotes on change is from John F. Kennedy:

> *Change is the law of life. And those who look only to the past or present are certain to miss the future.*

As is the law of nature, our ability to adapt to change determines our success. To that end, we seek out the tools and practices that will bring about that success. When it comes to books, there are a wide variety of books that describe the next new "approach" or "method," promising to improve efficiency and effectiveness if we just follow their prescription for success. Most of these models usually fall short because they fail to factor in the "ability to adapt" as a primary premise.

Getting Results the Agile Way has "adaptability" baked into the entire framework so you'll be able to factor in and manage changes when they happen instead of them managing you. One of the things I like most about the book is it has simple tools and techniques to help you break a problem down, determine the key outcomes, and think through what's most important to get done daily, weekly, and monthly—all without losing sight of the end game or your long term objectives. Having these great tools and practices that really work will help you to embrace change.

Although written for a wider audience, those of us in software development will find some of the concepts in the book familiar. With agile software development techniques, there are several core premises that we follow to make impact and get results. When we recognize we aren't getting the right result, we adapt and change our documented plan that is no longer working for us. If it has become out of date, we don't necessarily throw everything out, but we evaluate our standing plan. These Agile practices have become mainstream in the software development arena because they really help you get better results and have a greater impact.

Bottom line is it's all about the impact—not the activities. This is precisely where *Getting Results the Agile Way* can help.

I've seen J.D. Meier time and time again use the core principles outlined in *Getting Results the Agile Way* to deliver outstanding value which has had a positive impact for our customers and partners across the world. In the past, he has shared the approach with anyone who has asked. Now, he shares it with the rest of you. May you enjoy the rewards of bringing value, making an impact, and getting results!

Sincerely,

Michael Kropp
General Manager, Microsoft Corporation

A Word from the Author

Results was the name of the game, and I didn't have the playbook. When I first joined Microsoft more than 10 years ago, I was overwhelmed. It was a sink or swim environment. Every day I had to play catch up from the day before. I got more email than I could possibly read, more action items than I could possibly do, and challenges that were beyond my skills at the time. Inside the team, we affectionately called this scenario, "trial by fire." There were no boundaries to my days, each day bled into night, and I was consistently "burning the midnight oil." It reminded me of the saying, "Whatever doesn't kill you makes you stronger."

However, I hadn't moved across the country, leaving everything and everyone I knew behind, to fail right off the bat. One of the first things I did to survive was study the best of the best. I found people in the company that got results, and I learned from them. I learned everything I could about productivity from anybody who was willing to share their system with me.

I learned the **power of information management**. I was amazed how factoring out action from reference helped me cut my information overload. Simply getting organized helped me get unnecessary information out of my way, and helped me find the important information faster. By paying attention to how I used information, I could optimize for my main scenarios. For example, some things were "fire and forget" (i.e., deal with it now and be done), while others were "follow up." I was amazed at how much information I had optimized for look up, but never actually used.

I learned the **power of time management, focus, and prioritization**. Without time limits, I simply threw more hours at any problem: I treated time as my silver bullet, but I really was robbing Peter to pay Paul. I learned that by setting time limits on things like administration and email, I could better prioritize and focus. I learned to be accountable for my time.

I learned the **power of technique**. Without a technique, I couldn't consistently produce effective results. Of course, when I didn't have time limits, I didn't notice this because I simply threw more time at problems. Once I set limits, I had to find the most effective technique possible. For example, I found that keeping a simple list of actions outside of my email versus letting my inbox drive me, not only put me in control, but saved me countless wasted time and effort.

I learned the **power of project management**. When I moved to the patterns & practices team in Microsoft, my job went from working on smaller customer issues to driving projects and leading teams around the world. I had to learn how to break big problems down and make progress over time. I learned the impact of constraints in terms of time, resources, budget, and energy. I learned to play to my strengths, and how to maximize the impact of the overall team. Learning project management helped me learn the discipline of getting results on big problems spread over time.

I learned the **power of flexibility**. There's no one-size-fits-all, so I learned that I need to be flexible, and so does my system. I tested a lot of productivity systems. The problems I found with the systems I tried were that they were all or nothing, or they were too complicated, or they were tools-oriented, or they made me a slave to tasks and action items. I wanted to get out from under my backlogs, and I wanted agility and the ability to focus on opportunity. I stepped back and focused on the principles, patterns, and practices to integrate what I learned from productivity, project management, positive psychology, software development, and leadership skills.

Lastly, I learned the **power of balance**. When I was investing too much in work, I realized how that impacted other areas of my life. Through a lot of pain, trial and error, and feedback, I learned that I needed to treat life like a portfolio of investments. I could only spend my time and energy on so many things, but if I spent my time and energy in the right things, the sum became more than the parts. I learned to invest my life force in the following areas which I call **Hot Spots**: mind, body, emotions, career, financial, relationships, and fun. By investing in those buckets, while setting boundaries and limits, I've learned to find balance, while maximizing my results. The key to balance is to know these buckets and then invest wisely. The buckets support each other. Under-investing in one area, limits your results in other areas, just as over-investing in an area can take its toll. Balance and synergy are your friends.

As I mentored people and teams around Microsoft to help them get results, I honed my system. It was one thing for me to get results, but it has been quite another to package it up for other people. Because I was continuously building new project teams, I needed a system for getting new people on each team up to speed quickly. As the saying goes, "Necessity is the mother of invention." These challenges forced me to simplify my system, and lean it down to the most effective parts. The result is a time-tested system that scales up for large teams and down for individuals—it is a system I can bet on time and again. The most important thing is that it's simple, so if I fall off the horse, it's easy to get back on.

This guide is the playbook that I wish somebody had given me so many years ago for getting results.

—J.D.

Introduction

Agile means the ability to respond to change. In a changing world, your ability to learn and respond is one of your most crucial skills to go from surviving to thriving.

Agile Results® is a new, powerful system for getting results. It's a systematic way to achieve both short- and long-term results, and it works for all aspects of your life—from work to fun. This chapter introduces the guide, outlines its structure, and shows you how to apply the guidance to your specific needs.

The key to achieving results in today's world is agility. Traditional methods are static, and they just aren't working anymore. Agile Results provides just enough planning to get you going but makes it easy to change course as needed. This produces effective results by focusing on outcomes over activities.

About This Guide

This guide details a principle-based approach for getting results. Agile Results is designed with the big picture in mind, balancing work and life, while helping you live your values and play to your strengths. The guide provides end-to-end guidance for improving results on a daily, weekly, monthly, and yearly basis.

The following are some of the many ways to use this comprehensive guide:

- **A system for results.** Adopt the approach and practices that work for you and incorporate them into your daily routines.
- **A reference.** Use the guide as a reference and to learn principles, as well as patterns and practices for great results.
- **A mentor.** Use the guide as your mentor for learning how to achieve your objectives. The guide encapsulates the experience and lessons learned from many subject matter experts.

How This Guide Is Organized

Read this guide from beginning to end, or use it as a reference for specific needs. The guide is structured into three parts plus an appendix.

Part I, "Approach"

Part I provides an overview of the Agile Results approach, along with key values, principles, and practices. Hot Spots are introduced.

Part II, "Daily, Weekly, Monthly, Yearly Results"

Part II explains designing your day, week, month, and year using Agile Results.

Part III, "Results Explained"

Part III provides a solid foundation for results. It includes a set of guiding principles and key strategies for achieving results. It also explains the keys to motivation.

Appendix

This section provides step-by-step instructions and tools for turning the guidance into action.

How to Read This Guide

The following table shows a number of ways to get started.

Scenario	Approach
As a guide ...	Simply read the guide end-to-end.
As a reference ...	Flip to the back of the guide for the Appendix section, where you'll find cheat sheets, templates, and how-tos.
Take a test drive ...	Read "How To – Adopt Agile Results" and "How To – Adopt the 12 Core Practices of Agile Results" in the Appendix section of this guide.

This guide is really two books in one. The first section of this guide—Part I, II, and III—is intended to be read end-to-end; each chapter presents the big ideas, building on earlier concepts, and focuses on highlights. The second section of this guide—the Appendix—is an in-depth reference, providing specific, actionable guidance.

If you want to simply start test driving Agile Results, the best way is to start with "How To – Adopt Agile Results" in the Appendix section. It provides quick, step-by-step guidance for adopting the three key parts of Agile Results: (1) The Rule of 3; (2) Monday Vision, Daily Outcomes, Friday Reflection pattern; and (3) Hot Spots. Just by adopting these three parts, you can immediately start getting the benefits of work-life balance and focused results. This is the simplest way to get started and provides an incremental approach to adopting Agile Results.

If you want to explore key techniques in Agile Results, read "How To – Adopt the 12 Practices of Agile Results." You can adopt the practices incrementally, or better yet, this how-to describes a path that puts it all together.

Reading the book from beginning to end is, of course, the best way to get the most value from the guide. By understanding the motivation for the system first, you'll have that in the back of your mind as you read other material. Energy, motivation, and having a "Why" are important concepts found in this book; they can give you better footing in the system. The overview helps you understand the big picture and puts context to the procedures that come afterwards. "Chapter 1 – Why Agile Results?" presents the motivation for Agile Results, describing the problem it addresses and what makes it different and effective. When you read "Chapter 2 – Agile Results Overview," you'll have a good understanding of the main parts of Agile Results. When you read "Chapter 3 – Values, Principles, and Practices of Agile Results," you'll have a thorough understanding of the system. The rest of the guide provides support and detailed advice to ensure best results as you implement the system and integrate it into your life.

Part I – Approach

In This Part:

Chapter 1 – Why Agile Results?

Notice that the stiffest tree is most easily cracked, while the bamboo or willow survives by bending with the wind. —Bruce Lee

In This Chapter

- Learn how Agile Results is different from other systems.
- Learn how to improve your life with effective results.
- Learn the three keys to results.

This chapter explains how Agile Results differs from other systems you may have seen or tried, as well as what distinguishes it as effective for everything you apply it to. You can even apply Agile Results to your existing productivity system by applying the principles and practices.

Before going into the nuts and bolts of a solution, it's important to know the problem it solves and what sets it apart. Agile is the ability to respond to change. In a changing world, your ability to learn and respond is one of the most crucial skills to go from surviving to thriving. Agile Results is a flexible system for getting meaningful results. It's a cross-discipline approach for results that combines some of the most effective techniques in human performance for your mind, body, and emotions.

One of the most important concepts in Agile Results is the idea of agility. Maybe when you grew up, you thought you could go to school, learn a job, maybe switch careers once or twice, and then retire happily ever after. This big up-front design and long-term planning, just doesn't work in today's world. That doesn't mean give up planning. Instead, learn how to adjust your sails to the winds and tides and sail wherever it is you want to go with your life. Rethink your goals. Rather than a static set of dreams and ideals, test your results along the way and carve out the path that works for you. Mini-goals and actions go a long way towards your biggest and most impactful results.

Agile Results is elegance in action. It combines the art and the science of results. Don't let the simplicity fool you. It's been tested in some of the most complex working environments, as well as in private life.

The State of the Art vs. the State of the Practice

There are many state-of-the-art techniques people around the world are using every day to improve their results and amplify their impact. For example, sports psychologists have great techniques for improving the energy, focus and results of world class athletes. They even help athletes use stress to be their best. Highly effective project management techniques are available today for managing scope, estimating work, and scheduling. In software, Scrum and Agile practices are helping individuals and teams prioritize more effectively, get to working results faster, and respond to change.

Yet, the full potential of all this learning is rarely achieved in practice. There's a gap between the state of the art and the state of the practice. The state of the practice looks more like this:

- You can't keep up with change, and things are changing faster than ever.
- You don't finish what you start.
- What does get finished isn't what you actually wanted.
- You feel like there's never enough time.
- You regularly feel overwhelmed and drained.

The problem is, while you may learn a lot of things in school or on the job, you learn the least about the most important thing that can change your life. What's needed is an understanding of the art of results.

What Makes Agile Results Different?

What makes Agile Results different is that it integrates the world's best techniques for results.

1. **Outcomes over Activities.** Outcomes provide a lens for focus. Outcomes are the results you want to accomplish. Just doing more activities, checking off items from a task list, and throwing more time and energy at problems won't necessarily produce the results

you want. By starting with outcomes, you define what good will look like and you give yourself a compelling path to work towards. Working on the right things to produce the right results for your current situation is a recipe for success.

2. **Time as a First-Class Citizen.** In Agile Results, time is a first-class citizen. Windows of opportunity are important. It's about doing "good enough" for now, and versioning your results. Time changes what's important. What was important last month or last week might not be what's important now. That's the agile part— be responsive to what's important now. This also includes using timeboxes effectively. For example, rather than try to figure out how long something might take, start by figuring out how much time you want to invest in it. Identify up front at what point do diminishing returns become unacceptable. This will help you cut your losses and figure out how to optimize your time.

3. **Fresh Start.** If you fall off the horse, you can get back on. You get a fresh start each day, each week, each month, each year. What you take on is just as important as what you let go or "slough off." You don't want to be a beast of burden where one more straw breaks your back. It's about thinking in terms of delivering value over simply working through your backlog or crossing off a laundry list of to-dos. It's about asking and answering what's your next best thing to do.

4. **Test Your Results.** Have a bias for action. Rather than do a bunch of analysis and commit to a big plan up front, start taking action and testing you results. Use feedback to improve your plans. Testing your results is a way to find the risks and surprises earlier versus later. A simple way to remember this is "Do it, review it, and improve it." In addition, you'll find that action creates inspiration. A lot of people wait for their moment of inspiration before they start, but what they don't realize is that simply by starting, the inspiration can follow. It's like going to see a movie and then enjoying it more than you expected.

5. **Fix Time, Flex Scope.** By fixing time, you set yourself up for success. The main thing is to set a fixed time for eating, sleeping, and working out. You can also fix time within work. For example, you can decide that work is an eight hour day within which you set timeboxes to produce results: an hour for administration, four hours for execution, two hours for think time, and a minimum of an hour on communication and relationships.

At a higher level, you might fix time to be a 40-hour or 50-hour work week. Within that time frame, you will bite off the work you can do. What you won't do is flex time. You won't throw more hours at the problem each day. You'll gradually learn to bite off what you can accomplish and manage your plate more effectively.

6. **Boundaries.** Boundaries are simply minimums and maximums. Setting boundaries is a key to success. You'll produce more effective results by spending the right time and energy on the right things. You can set boundaries with time; for example, tell yourself, "I'll spend no more than an hour on that." You can set boundaries in terms of energy; for example, tell yourself, "I'll stop when I start to feel tired." Most people trip up by not setting boundaries. They'll work on something until they crash. They throw all their time in one area at the expense of other areas. Setting boundaries is how you can add balance to your life. You can spread your time and energy across the important Hot Spots.

7. **Tests for Success.** Your tests for success answer the question, "What will good look like?" Simply by figuring out the three outcomes you want for the day, the week, the month, and the year, you identify your tests for success. You have an idea of what you want to accomplish and what good will look like. Knowing your tests for success helps you prioritize.

8. **Approach over Results.** How you accomplish your results is more important than the results themselves in the long run. Your approach is your foundation. It's what you fall back on when you don't know the way forward. Your approach should be sustainable. You should also be able to improve your approach over time. Your approach should be consistent with your values. Your approach should play to your strengths and limit your weaknesses.

9. **The Rhythm of Results.** Iterate on your results. Version your results over time. The rhythm of results is your daily, weekly, monthly, and yearly results. This is about flowing value incrementally. Think of it as a set of trains that come and go from the station. If you miss a train, you can catch the next one. At the same time, you want to catch certain trains because of your time frames and windows of opportunity.

10. **Time, Energy, and Technique.** You don't want to just throw more time at problems. You also don't want to burn yourself out

by just throwing your energy into things. Your results are a combination of time, energy, and technique. By using more effective techniques, you can amplify your results. This is how you use your time and energy more effectively.

11. **Strengths over Weaknesses.** Rather than spend all your time improving your weaknesses, spend your time playing to your strengths. While it's important to reduce your liabilities, you'll go further, have more passion, and produce more effective results by spending more time in your strengths. In areas that you are weak, one of your best moves is to partner or team up with others that supplement you. If you can't outsource your weaknesses, you can find more effective mentors or pair up with other people who help you amplify your results.

12. **System over Ad Hoc.** When you have routines for how you produce results, you can learn and improve. It's one thing to produce results randomly, while it's another to have a system you can count on. When you have a system, you can tune and prune what works for you.

13. **Continuous Learning.** The world's not static. Skills aren't static. You're not static. Learning is a first-class citizen. It's about taking action, getting the feedback, and changing your approach. It's about letting go of what's not working, and testing new ways to achieve your results. It's about personalizing your approach and continuously refining it to meet your needs. Your weekly reflection will help you learn more about yourself in terms of your strengths, your weaknesses, your passions, your bottlenecks, and ultimately your results. While improving your results, you'll improve the way you produce results. Improving the way you produce results, will improve your enjoyment and fulfillment no matter what you work on.

In the next chapters, you'll see the "What" and "How" behind Agile Results. You'll see how to achieve your best results by combining the power of multiple patterns and practices.

Life's Better with Results

When you lead a life of results, you make things happen. Whether it's getting your body in shape, achieving excellence at work, or just getting things done around the house, results is the name of the game.

Sometimes having fun is the result you want, and Agile Results helps you with that too. Knowing how to produce results effectively and efficiently, changes your game. Here are some examples of how Agile Results can work for you:

- You find your flow and are focused and engaged in whatever you do.
- You learn the best ways of doing things over time and avoid painful pitfalls.
- You're responsive to change and have unlimited energy to take on whatever life throws your way.
- You have a rhythm of results that helps you get up to bat time and again.
- You play to your strengths and live your values.
- You regularly enjoy power hours and creative hours to unleash your best results.
- You find your best work-life balance.
- You spend less time working but produce more effective results.

The Way of Results

The way of results is moving forward. It's growth over decline. It's learning over failing. It's outcomes over activities. It's meaningful results. It's valuing your time. It's taking action. It's balancing your demands. It's having an enjoyable journey towards a compelling end in mind. You get more out of life when you know what you want to get. You get more out of life when you have a sustainable approach. The key is a flexible approach that supports you.

3 Keys to Results

You can master your time management only to spend your time on the wrong things. You can master task management and miss windows of opportunity. What are the real keys to results?

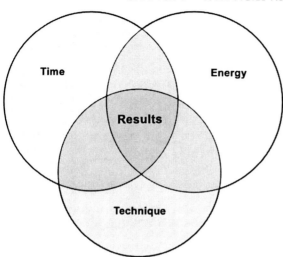

Figure 1.1
3 Keys to Results

There are three keys that can change your game pretty quickly.

Key 1. The Key to Time Management Is Energy Management

Managing your energy is how you produce more results in the same amount of time. You don't get more hours in a day, but you can change your level of energy. If you can spend more time in your power hours or add more power hours to your week, you improve your results.

Key 2. The Key to Energy Management Is Passion

Living with passion is a key to your best results. When you think about energy, think of your mind, body, and emotions. You can eat right, sleep like a baby, and get ripped at the gym. In contrast, you can get physically drained, mentally drained, or emotionally drained. Your energy depends on fulfilling your passions. Your mind, body, and emotions play off each other.

Key 3. The Key to Results Is Time, Energy and Technique

The key to results is using your time and energy more effectively and efficiently. You can't just throw time at problems. If you throw time at a problem, but you don't have enough energy, you can spend way more time than you need to. On the other hand, if you have a lot of energy, and you throw time at the problem, but you don't have the right technique, you can churn and burn, but never actually get the results you want. The key is to spend your time working on the right things with your best energy and the best techniques.

The three keys of results are shifts in thinking. For example, if you've approached productivity as simply managing time, then you've missed out on the benefits of managing energy. If you've tackled productivity as an exercise in task management, then you've potentially missed out on producing meaningful results or playing to your passions. If you've thrown time and energy at problems, but you didn't focus on exploring your techniques, there's a good chance that you can get back a lot of time and energy each week, simply by swapping out for more effective techniques.

You will see how to apply these keys throughout this guide.

In Summary

- Agile Results is a personal productivity system that combines the best patterns and practices from a variety of disciplines.
- There is a gap between the state of the art and the state of the practice when it comes to results.
- Agile Results has a special emphasis on simplicity.
- There are three keys to results: (1) improve your results by improving your energy; (2) spend more time in your passion to improve your energy; and (3) combine time, energy, and technique for your most effective results.

Chapter 2 – Agile Results Overview

You see, in life, lots of people know what to do, but few people actually do what they know. Knowing is not enough! You must take action. —Tony Robbins

In This Chapter

- Learn the basics of the Agile Results system.
- Learn how to map out important areas of your work and life so you can invest your time and energy more effectively.
- Learn a pattern for weekly results.

This chapter provides an overview of the Agile Results system.

Agile Results is a system for results. It's a simple system optimized around time. It's a collection of principles, patterns, and practices for getting results. It draws from lessons learned as well as from bodies of knowledge in project management, software engineering, and personal development. Here are the key parts of the system:

- **The Rule of 3.** This is a guideline that helps you prioritize and scope. Rather than bite off more than you can chew, you bite off three things. You can use The Rule of 3 at different levels by picking three outcomes for the day, the week, the month, and the year. This helps you see the forest from the trees since your three outcomes for the year are at a higher level than your three outcomes for the month, and your three outcomes for the week are at a higher level than your three outcomes for the day.
- **Monday Vision, Daily Outcomes, Friday Reflection.** This is a simple time-based pattern. Each week is a fresh start. On Mondays, you think about three outcomes you would like for the week. Each day you identify three outcomes you would like for the day. On Fridays, you reflect on lessons learned; you ask yourself, "What three things are going well, and what three things need improvement?" This weekly pattern helps you build momentum.
- **Hot Spots.** Hot Spots help you map out your results. They are the key levers in the system. They're your lens to help you focus

on what's important in your life. They can represent areas of opportunity or pain. Hot Spots are your main dashboard. It helps to organize your Hot Spots by work, personal, and life. At a glance, you should be able to quickly see the balls you're juggling and what's on your plate. To find your Hot Spots, simply make a list of the key areas that need your time and energy. Then for each of these key areas, it's important to have scannable outcomes—a tickler list that easily answers the question, "What do you want to accomplish?" When you know the results you want in your Hot Spots for your work and personal life, you have a map for your results.

You can use Agile Results for work or home or anywhere you need to improve your results in life. Agile Results is compatible with and can enhance the results of any productivity system you already use.

Agile Results at a Glance

This is a bird's-eye view of Agile Results.

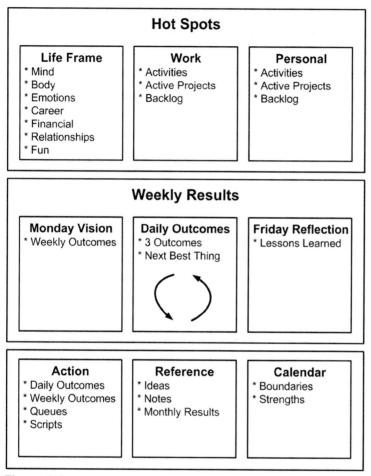

Figure 2.1
Agile Results at a Glance

As mentioned earlier in the guide, Agile Results is a system for work and life. It's an adaptable productivity system focused on outcomes over activities. It's taking action towards compelling outcomes and producing incremental results. It's being flexible and responsive to change. Creating outcomes is an important concept in Agile Results. They guide your actions. Think of it as working backwards, always mindful of your objectives. This is a sharp contrast from focusing on tasks or task management. While tasks are important, if you focus on the end game, you will find a way there. The key to success is looking ahead just enough to know that the next vital few things you do, contribute to the results you want to accomplish. A shift in thinking about time is required. In Agile Results, you fix time and flex scope. This means you set a fixed amount of time for your results each day. You then bite off only what you can chew.

Agile Results is not a checklist of things to do. It's not a way to do "more stuff" in your life. It's a way to balance what's important, respond to a changing world, live your values, and spend more time doing what you love, while improving your efficiency and effectiveness.

Hot Spots

Hot Spots are key areas that deserve your attention. These could be areas of opportunity or they could be pain points. Either way, they are areas that need your time, energy, and focus.

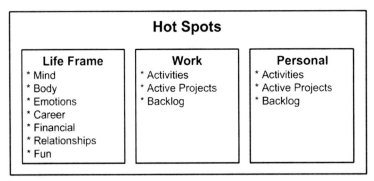

Figure 2.2
Hot Spots

These could be reflected in projects or simply as either work streams or activities. What's important is to know at a glance what your Hot Spots are and what you want to accomplish. At a high level, you can think in terms of life, work, and personal. Scannability is important— think of tickler lists where each item is just enough information to remind you. This is a key for agility.

Invest in Your Hot Spots

Invest your time and energy across your Hot Spots. Balance is important since Hot Spots tend to support each other. For example, investing in your mind and body helps with your emotions; investing in your relationships can help with your career. Likewise, Hot Spots can also negatively impact one another. For example, over-investing in your career can damage your relationships; ignoring your body can hamper your fun. You can use Hot Spots as a frame for reflection to keep a gauge on your success. In each of these Hot Spots, you're either growing or dying. Ideally, you find a way so that it gets easier to amplify your results across the Hot Spots. For example, in the right job, working with the right people, on the right things, making the right impact can take care of several of your Hot Spots. In contrast, if you're not in the right job, you might find yourself working extra hard to grow your mind, keep your emotions in check, and have fun.

Life Frame

The Life Frame is a set of Hot Spots for life. They are a set of categories that tend to be important for continuous success. You can think of them as a portfolio of results:

- Mind
- Body
- Emotions
- Career
- Financial
- Relationships
- Fun

Mind includes investing time in learning thinking techniques and keeping your mind sharp. Body includes investing time in keeping your body in shape and learning patterns and practices for health; the basics are eating, sleeping, and working out. The Emotions category includes investing time to keep your emotions healthy, learn emotional intelligence, and keep your emotions in check; it's about learning skills for feeling good. Career includes your job and professional activities. The Financial category includes investing time to learn patterns and practices for building and sustaining wealth. The Relationships category includes relationships at home, work, and life. Fun includes investing time to play and do whatever you enjoy.

Work Hot Spots

If you don't work for a living, congratulations, you can skip this part. Otherwise, focus on these areas to get crisp at work:

- Activities
- Active Projects
- Backlog

Activities are anything you need to spend your time and energy on. Active projects are the work projects that you are actively working on. Anything you're not actively working on, but you plan to, is your backlog. For your active projects, a simple thing to do is make a simple list for each of your active projects. This gives you a place to write down important outcomes. You can do the same for your backlog: make one list for each backlog project. By having a list, you have a place to put things, rather than have them float around in your head. You know you have a good set of lists when you can quickly tell at a glance what your current projects are. If you aren't used to thinking in terms of projects, you can simply think of all the balls you are currently juggling at work. In each project list, you should see a set of outcomes at a glance. The outcomes will help you see the forest from the trees.

Personal Hot Spots

These are your personal projects and things you spend time on outside of work:

- Activities
- Active Items
- Backlog

Activities are anything from a recurring task to things you need to spend your time and energy on; these are the balls you are juggling at home. Active Projects are the personal projects you are actively working on; this could be anything from writing a book to fixing the house. Backlog is the list of projects you plan to do but aren't actually working on.

Monday Vision, Daily Outcomes, Friday Reflection

This figure shows a simple pattern for weekly results.

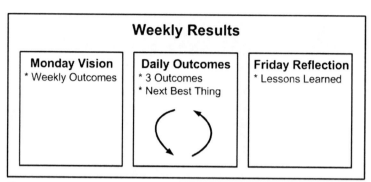

Figure 2.3
Monday Vision, Daily Outcomes, Friday Reflection

On Mondays, identify three compelling results you'd like for the week. Each day identify three key results for the day; your three outcomes for the week will help guide you. This is The Rule of 3; it's easy to remember three things and also easy to prioritize three things. Then on Fridays, you reflect on your accomplishments.

Monday Vision

Each Monday is a fresh start to a new week. It's your chance to define what a good week will look like. You can then carve out the results to help you get there. A simple way to accomplish this is to ask yourself, "If this were Friday, what are the three most important results that I want to have under my belt?" Here are the keys to Monday Vision:

- Each Monday, identify the most important outcomes for the week.
- Take the time to see the forest from the trees.
- Use The Rule of 3 to help you narrow down to the three most important outcomes for the week.

Daily Outcomes

Ultimately, this is the guiding question, "What three things do I want to accomplish today?"

If you do nothing else, simply write down or remember three of your most important outcomes for the day. The benefit of writing down your list is that it gives you a place to dump things so that you don't fill your head with noise. Writing things down can also help put things in perspective.

Ideally, start by listing your MUST items. Next, list any of your SHOULD or COULD items. Then, use The Rule of 3 to bubble up what's most important. Rather than think of it as backlog burndown, think in terms of value up—each day is a new opportunity to deliver value. Value can be for yourself or others. Remember that value is in the eye of the beholder. Each day, is a clean slate.

Note that even if you already have a to-do system, you can use whatever is already working for you. Simply add your three outcomes to the top. Now, whenever you look at your to-do list, you have your tests for success. Your three outcomes will help guide you and help you prioritize your actions and tasks against the results you want to achieve.

Here are the key things to keep in mind:
- Identify three outcomes for the day. These are the results you've chosen as the most important and will therefore get the laser-like focus they deserve.
- Name your list using today's date (e.g., 2010-01-11).
- As you fish your various streams for potential actions, be mindful of your three outcomes. (Your streams include meetings, email, conversations, or bursts of brilliance throughout the day.)
- Adjust your outcomes as appropriate.

There are several benefits to using Daily Outcomes. While it seems simple, it's actually combining simplicity with focus, prioritization, and a conscious choice around value and results. You get a fresh start each day. Each day, you focus on the most valuable things (whether for you, your job, or other people). You decide on what to carry forward each day. Rather than base your day on things you didn't get done in the past, you base your day on what you want to accomplish and on what has the most impact or value for you at this point in time. Lower priority or lower value naturally sloughs off. It's lightweight and works whether you use pen and paper, a whiteboard, or store things electronically.

Friday Reflection

One of the most important things you start to learn is your actual capacity. The more you check your results, the more you will learn to adjust your own expectations, as well as set expectations more effectively with others. Friday is a great day to reflect back on your week. Here are the key things:

- Evaluate what you accomplished, or didn't, and why.
- Identify three things that went well.
- Identify three things that need improvement.
- Evaluate your energy levels.
- Carry your lessons forward to your next Monday Vision.

A good reflection system is not simply listing three things going well and three things to improve. It's taking the time to use it as a true learning session. It's your chance to identify things that you want to stop doing, as well as things that you want to start doing, based on your results. Over time, weekly reinforcement will make a substantial difference. It's a process of continuous improvement that helps you refine your overall process for results. This simple process can have amazing impact across your work and life, especially if you're using the time to really hone in on what's working, what's not, and change your approach. Remember that each week is a fresh start, and each day is another chance to get up to bat.

Action

Factoring your actions from your reference information is one of the simplest moves to improve your results.

Figure 2.4
Action

This is especially true if you tend to have a lot of tickler lists and reminders that are really more notes than actions. Reference is simply input for you. If you have to filter through a bunch of reference to find your actions, the friction adds up. Instead, it's better to have a home for action items and a home for reference items.

Here's a summary of each type of information around action items and taking action:

- Daily Outcomes
- Weekly Outcomes
- Queues
- Scripts

Daily Outcomes is the tickler list of outcomes that you create each day as part of your Monday Vision, Daily Outcomes, Friday Reflection. Queues are the tickler lists of outcomes and tasks that you created for each of the significant projects and key activities identified for your Hot Spots. This is input for your Daily Outcomes list; it's also a place to put things that you won't get done for the day, but that you need to remember. Scripts is your repository for step-by-step instructions; each script is a list of steps in sequence to help you perform a task. Think of it as putting your routines down into writing. By having them written down, you can make it easier to perform a task each time instead of trying to remember what to do, especially when a task is done infrequently. You can also use it as a baseline for improvement by sharing your script with others and getting feedback. Another benefit is that it saves time should you have to delegate the task to others.

Reference

Think of reference as information that you need to refer to.

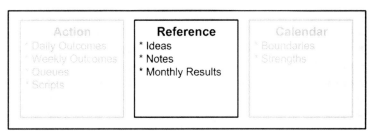

Action	Reference	Calendar
* Daily Outcomes	* Ideas	* Boundaries
* Weekly Outcomes	* Notes	* Strengths
* Queues	* Monthly Results	
* Scripts		

Figure 2.5
Reference

It may help you perform your action items but it's not actually actionable information. For example, your to-do list would be your actions, but supporting information would be your reference. You can use collection pools to consolidate and organize your reference information. Consider having a single place to consolidate your ideas, notes, and results. Also consider making a simple way to scan your weekly and monthly results to make sure that you're moving in the direction you want to go. Here are some examples of collection pools:

• Ideas
• Notes
• Monthly Results

Ideas is a repository for your ideas. Notes are tickler lists of insights or data points or anything you need to refer to as your notes. Weekly Results are tickler lists of actual results accomplished for each week. Monthly Results are tickler lists of actual results accomplished each month. Use the Weekly Results and Monthly Results to keep score. For example, for your Weekly Outcomes, list the three outcomes you want for the week on Monday; then on Friday, list your actual results as Weekly Results. Do the same thing for your Monthly Outcomes and Monthly Results. It's a great way to keep track of your progress; it also comes in handy if you need to report your status to someone else.

Calendar

Carve out time for what's important. Your calendar is one of your most important tools. It's how you organize your time.

Figure 2.6
Calendar

It's easy to fall into routines simply by how, where, and when you spend your time. If you don't drive your calendar, your calendar drives you. The beauty is that once you've organized your calendar in a way that supports you, you have more energy for everything you do and you get to recharge. Remember it's not doing less that makes you feel better or stronger. It's spending more time in your strengths and following your passions, and less time doing things that make you weak. The more time you spend in your strengths, the more energy you will have. The more energy you have the more you can accomplish with less effort and less churn.

Here are the key things to keep in mind:
- Schedule your results.
- Block time for what's important.
- Make (and keep) appointments with yourself; schedule time for execution or think time as you need it.
- Spend more time in your strengths than in your weaknesses.
- Balance is your friend.

The Rhythm of Results

Having a rhythm for your results helps you build routines and improve your ability to get results.

Daily, Weekly, Monthly Results

Think of the rhythm of results in terms of daily, weekly, and monthly results. Use The Rule of 3 to accomplish three meaningful results each day, each week, and each month. The results add up fast. Most importantly, it's a very simple way to frame out results. Rather than get caught up in the details, it's easy to step back and think in terms of three items. Then, whether you're looking at a day, a week or a month, you can quickly look at the bigger picture. For example, the three results for the month are at a much higher level than the three outcomes for the week, which are much higher than the outcomes for each day. It's a quick way to traverse a lot of action that's spread over time while not getting bogged down in the tasks themselves. It's an incremental sketch of your results, rendered daily, weekly, and monthly.

In Summary

- Invest your time and energy across your Hot Spots.
- The Life Frame is a set of Hot Spots for life: mind, body, emotions, career, financial, relationships, and fun.
- Monday Vision, Daily Outcomes, Friday Reflection is a pattern for weekly results.
- On Mondays, identify three key results you want for the week.
- Each day, identify three key results you want for the day.
- On Fridays, think of three things going well and three things to improve.
- Factor action from reference information.
- Design your weekly schedule so that you make time for what's important and you balance across your Hot Spots.

Chapter 3 –
Values, Principles, and Practices of Agile Results

Absorb what is useful. Discard what is not. Add what is uniquely your own. —Bruce Lee

In This Chapter
- Learn the key values of Agile Results.
- Learn the key principles of Agile Results.
- Learn the key practices of Agile Results.

The foundation for Agile Results is a set of 10 values, 10 principles, and 12 practices. One way to think of the Agile Results approach is that it's an iterative and incremental system for producing results in your life. Rather than big, up-front design, it's about paving a path and finding a way forward. Agile Results is optimized for responding to change. It's a flexible system that you can tune or tailor as needed.

The values provide insight into how I shaped Agile Results into a system, including the trade-offs I made. The principles are guidelines. Whenever I come to a fork in the road, the principles help me choose a path. The core practices are a simple set of methods and techniques for implementing Agile Results; they transform the principles and values into action. The supporting practices (found in "Cheat Sheet – Supporting Practices Defined") provide additional tools for success.

You don't have to adopt all the practices at once. Agile Results is flexible. Simply adopt the practices you need. And you can adopt them one at a time. A minimal implementation is simple. Use The Rule of 3 to decide three results you want to accomplish today. Dedicate laser-like focus to achieving these three results. If you find yourself distracted by another focus, ask yourself whether that should be the next best thing to do. If so, perhaps you should swap it for one of your initial three results. If not, consider resetting your focus to one of the three which you've defined as the most important outcomes of the day. These three are either the most important outcomes for your day, or they're not. It's your call. Next, adopt the Monday Vision,

Daily Outcomes, Friday Reflection pattern: use Monday Vision to define three outcomes for the week; focus each day on three Daily Outcomes (many of which will drive your three weekly outcomes); and use Friday Reflection to analyze what worked and what didn't. Adopting this pattern, you have a means for achieving daily, weekly, monthly, and yearly results. Next, adopt the Hot Spots. Though Hot Spots are an integral part of Agile Results, you don't need to pay full attention to them to get started. As you establish a rhythm of results, improve your rhythm by adopting new practices, learning your own strengths and weaknesses, and making adjustments which work best for you. Indeed, it's a lifetime pattern for results and success.

10 Values

Values set the stage. Values are a way to help make trade-offs when there are a lot of options and possibilities. An effective system uses values to help guide and identify relevant principles and practices. Here are the key values in Agile Results:

1. **Action over Analysis Paralysis.** Taking action is the best antidote for analysis paralysis. Rather than over-engineer or try to figure out everything up front, start taking action. Your results will inform your thinking, and you can change your course as needed.

2. **Approach over Results.** You can't control your results. You can control your attitude, actions, and response. Use your results as a gauge and for feedback.

3. **Energy over Time.** Focus on keeping your energy strong. You'll get more done in one power hour than throwing lots of hours at a problem when you just don't have the energy. In addition to eating right, sleeping well, and working out, the key to energy is following your passion and living your values.

4. **Focus over Quantity.** It's not about doing more. It's about focusing on the right things. Focus is your force multiplier.

5. **Good Enough over Perfection.** Don't let perfectionism get in the way. It's better to produce something that you can improve or iterate on, than to continuously block yourself while striving for perfection.

6. **Growth Mindset over Fixed Mindset.** A growth mindset means that you can learn and respond. A fixed mindset means that you think something was born that way and won't change. By adopting a growth mindset, you help avoid learned helplessness.

You also pay more attention to your situation and feedback. You also become more flexible in your approach. This flexibility is your key to results. It's how you will improve over time.

7. **Outcomes over Activities.** Spending more time or doing more things isn't a good measure of productivity. Results are the best measure. By focusing on your results instead of your activities, you can place value on where you spend your time. By getting clarity on what you want to accomplish, you can be flexible in your approach.
8. **Strengths over Weaknesses.** Spend more time in your strengths than in your weaknesses. Rather than spend all your energy improving your weaknesses, spend your energy maximizing your strengths. You'll get more payback. If you do work on your weaknesses, then focus on reducing your key liabilities.
9. **System over Ad Hoc.** Having a system for results is a powerful thing. It gives you a firm foundation. You can experiment more. When you get off track, you have something to fall back on or to turn to when you need it. By having a system for the basics, you can move yourself up the stack and automatically invest yourself in higher level matters. Most importantly, you free your mind by having trusted places to look and a trusted process to fall back on.
10. **Value Up over Backlog Burndown.** Rather than just work through your backlog, think in terms of creating value. This can be value for yourself, other people, or your employer. This is a value-up strategy. By thinking in terms of value up, you get in the habit of asking, "What's the next best thing to do?"

10 Principles

Principles are simply a set of guiding rules. Here are the key principles for Agile Results:

1. **80/20 Action.** Rather than spend 80 percent stuck in analysis and only 20 percent doing, it's about shifting to spend 80 percent of your time in action.
2. **Change Your Approach.** Tune and adjust as you go. If it's not working, let it go.
3. **Continuous Learning.** As you change and as things change around you, use your learning to improve your results.
4. **Deliver Incremental Value.** Find a way to flow value. Chunking up your results helps you build momentum. It also helps

you build credibility with yourself and others. Rather than wait for a big bang at the end, you can flow value.

5. **Less Is More.** Bite off what you can chew and reduce work that's in flight.

6. **Factor Action from Reference.** You should keep your action items separate from reference. This helps reduce the signal-to-noise ratio.

7. **Set Boundaries.** Set boundaries in terms of time or energy. Consider boundaries for the following Hot Spots: mind, body, emotions, career, financial, relationships, and fun. The key is to have a minimum in some categories and a maximum in others.

8. **Fix Time, Flex Scope.** Treat time as a first-class citizen. First set time boundaries. Next, bite off what you can chew within those boundaries.

9. **Rhythm of Results.** Focus on daily, weekly, monthly, and yearly results. Building a rhythm builds a habit that you don't have to think about. The habit becomes a ritual that produces a feeling of accomplishment.

10. **Version Your Results.** You can improve your results on each pass. Version 3 will be better than version 2 which will be better than version 1. This helps you fight perfectionism and produce incremental results.

12 Core Practices of Agile Results

At the heart of any system is a set of practices. It's the practices that make or break a system. Combined with the 10 values and 10 principles, the 12 core practices complete the foundation of Agile Results:

1. **The Rule of 3.** This is the heart of your Daily Outcomes. The Rule of 3 will help you stay focused on the vital few things that matter. Identify your three key outcomes each day, each week, each month, and each year. This helps you see the forest from the trees. The three outcomes for the year are bigger than the three outcomes for the month which are bigger than the three outcomes for the week which are bigger than the three outcomes for your day. This also helps you manage scope. It's all too easy to bite off more than you can chew. Instead, first nail the three items you want to accomplish, and then bite off more. Think of it as a buffet

of results and you can keep going back—just don't overflow your plate on each trip.

2. **Monday Vision, Daily Outcomes, Friday Reflection.** Decide three results you want to accomplish for the week. Decide what three results you want to accomplish each day. Make progress each day. At the end of the week, reflect on your results.

3. **Scannable Outcomes.** Think of this as what's on your radar. At a glance, you should be able to see what you want to accomplish and what you're spending your time and energy on. Outcomes guide your actions. Keep your outcomes scannable at a glance. Organize outcomes by your work, personal, and life Hot Spots. For example, create a list of outcomes for your Life Frame Hot Spots: body, career, emotions, financial, fun, mind, and relationships.

4. **Daily Outcomes.** Each day is a new chance for results. Use daily tickler lists for action items; create a new list each day. Each day, decide on three things you want to accomplish (The Rule of 3). Always start your list with your three most important outcomes for the day. The key to an effective Daily Outcomes list is that you keep your three outcomes for the day at the top, while listing the rest of your to-dos below that. This way you have a reminder of what you want to accomplish.

5. **Weekly Outcomes.** Create a new list each week. Each week is a new chance for results. Always start with your three most important outcomes for the week (The Rule of 3).

6. **Strong Week.** Each week focus on spending more time on activities that make you strong and less time on activities that make you weak. Push activities that make you weak to the first part of your day. By doing your worst things first, you create a glide path for the rest of the day. Set limits; stuff the things that make you weak into a timebox. For example, if the stuff that makes you weak is taking more than 20 percent of your day, then find a way to keep it within that 20 percent boundary. This might mean limiting the time or quantity. Sometimes you just can't get rid of the things that make you weak; in that case, balance it with more things that energize you and make you strong. Apply this to your week too. Push the toughest things that drain you to the start of the week to create a glide path. Do the same with people. Spend more time with people that make you strong and less time with people that make you weak. Be careful not to confuse the things

that make you weak with challenges that will actually make you stronger. Grow yourself stronger over time.

7. **Timebox Your Day.** Set boundaries for how much time you spend on things. If you keep time a constant (by ending your day at a certain time), it helps you figure out where to optimize your day and prioritize. To start, you can carve up your day into big buckets: administration, work time, think time, and people time.

8. **Triage.** Triage incoming action items to either do it, queue it, schedule it, or delegate it. Do it if now is the time: it's the next best thing for you to do; now is the most opportunistic time; or it will cost you more pain, time or effort to do it later. Queue it (add it to your queue) if it's something you need to get done, but now is not the right time. Schedule it if you need a block of time to get the work done. Delegate it if it's something that should be done by somebody else.

9. **Monthly Improvement Sprints.** Pick one thing to improve for the month. Each month, pick something new; this gives you a chance to cycle through 12 things over the year. Or if necessary, you can always repeat a sprint. The idea is that 30 days is enough time to experiment with your results throughout the month. Because you might not see progress in the first couple of weeks while you're learning, a month is a good chunk of time to check your progress.

10. **Growth Mindset.** This is simply a decision—decide that you'll learn and grow. If you get knocked down, you'll get up again. You decide that no problem is personal, pervasive or permanent. Life is not static. Neither are your results.

11. **Action Lists.** Track your actions with tickler lists. Consider the following action lists: Daily Outcomes, Weekly Outcomes, Queues, and Scripts.

12. **Reference Collections.** Some information is not actionable. Yes, it might be helpful information, and yes, it might be good to know. But if it's not actionable, then it's reference. You can store your reference information as tickler lists or notes. Here are some example reference lists you might keep: Ideas, Notes, Weekly Results, Monthly Results, and Yearly Results.

The 12 core practices are part of the foundation of Agile Results. Remember to check out the supporting practices; they provide additional tools for success. To see a list of these supporting practices along with their description, see "Cheat Sheet – Supporting Practices Defined" in the Appendix section of this guide.

In Summary

- Tailor and adapt Agile Results to suit your own needs; it's flexible by design.
- Knowing the values helps you understand the priorities and trade-offs of the Agile Results system. The principles are guidelines which help you make choices.
- You don't have to adopt Agile Results all at once; you can adopt the Agile Results practices incrementally. Use the values, principles, and practices as a starting point.
- The simplest way to get started with Agile Results is to adopt The Rule of 3 and identify three results you want to accomplish for today. Next, adopt the Monday Vision, Daily Outcomes, Friday Reflection pattern to help you achieve weekly results. Next, adopt Hot Spots to help achieve a balanced life.

Chapter 4 – Hot Spots

One reason so few of us achieves what we truly want is that we never direct our focus; we never concentrate our power. — Tony Robbins

In This Chapter

- Learn how to use Hot Spots to focus and invest your time and energy in major areas of your life.
- Learn how to use Hot Spots to set boundaries to improve your work-life balance.
- Learn how to invest in your relationships more effectively.

This chapter is an elaboration and drill down into the concept of Hot Spots as it applies to Agile Results.

Hot Spots help shine the spotlight on things that are important. The primary goal of using Hot Spots is to have a quick way to identify, organize and scan what's important. Start by identifying your most important Hot Spots for work, personal, and life. Next, explicitly name the outcomes you want for each of these Hot Spots. Finally, create "scannable outcomes" so you can see at a glance your Hot Spots and desired outcomes. Knowing the results you want for your Hot Spots forces you to get clarity. Keeping them simple and scannable, like a tickler list, makes it easy to update your goals and aspirations as they change. That's the agile part. What's important will change as you learn more and gain clarity or adjust to new situations. Time has a way of changing what's important now.

By having a simple set of Hot Spots, you have a way to keep your life in check. By investing across your Hot Spots, you keep your life in balance and you invest in yourself for the long run. The key is setting boundaries. To set boundaries, simply identify minimums and maximums where you need them. Factoring the Hot Spots out is a way to help you focus and get clarity on where a particular dimension of your life is at. Remember that the sum is more than the parts and that the Hot Spots actually support each other.

Hot Spots

Where do you need to spend your time? What do you need to focus on? Hot Spots is a simple metaphor for thinking about what's important.

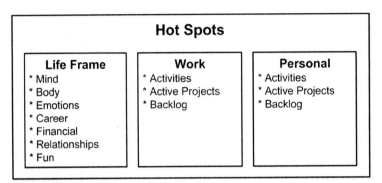

Figure 4.1
Hot Spots

It's where the action is or should be. More importantly, it's where your attention, energy, and focus should be. Imagine your Hot Spots as a heat map, a bird's-eye view of what's important. Heat maps are often used in the military to show clusters of important activity. For your heat map, simply visualize the clusters of important things going on in your life. The heat map can show either opportunities or pain points. On the opportunity side, you can imagine new interests, business ideas, or potential game changers. On the pain side, you can imagine areas that you've neglected and are now causing you pain physically, emotionally, financially, etc. You can also imagine areas that have a lot of friction. Maybe they are just a little tougher than they should be, and maybe a bit of focus would help you unblock results in these Hot Spots.

See the Forest from the Trees

When you're in the thick of things, it can be tough to see the bigger picture. This is especially true if you don't know what to look for. Hot Spots can help you see the forest from the trees in a few ways. For example, at the macro level, you can think of Hot Spots in terms of work, personal, and life. You can think of your life Hot Spots in terms of mind, body, emotions, career, financial, relationships, and fun. Within each of those Hot Spots, you can then identify the main things that are important for you. You can do the same for work and personal; if you aren't sure where to start, you can at least think of your work and personal Hot Spots in terms of your projects, activities, and roles for each.

Hot Spots as Your Heat Map

As a heat map, your Hot Spots help you answer the question, "What's on your radar?" You don't need to know all the details, and your map doesn't need to be complete. In fact, that would actually get in the way. You would either spend all your time updating the map to be complete or bury what's important among the details. Instead, you need to know your main threats and opportunities. At a high level, your primary threats are things that negatively impact your mind, body, emotions, career, financial, relationships, and fun. Your opportunities are things that will add value or improve your life in these areas. At a lower level, look for the big threats and opportunities in your work projects and activities as well as your personal projects and activities. Your heat map of Hot Spots let's you take a step back. You want to avoid getting blind-sided or over-investing in one area at the expense of another. You also want to avoid spending all your time fighting fires while missing out on opportunities. When you know where to look, it's easier to gain insight. You can start to see patterns. You get a better lens for what's working and what's not. When you know what to look for, you can figure out which levers matter most. You want to find the right levers to either get unstuck or maximize your results. You should be able to know at a glance where the pain or opportunity is.

Hot Spots as Your Portfolio

Your Hot Spots is your investment portfolio, and the goal is to more thoughtfully spread your life force across this portfolio. You already spend your time and energy on a variety of things. Hot Spots help you answer the question, "Where should you invest your time for maximum results?" When you think of your results as a portfolio, it helps you manage risk. You might be over-investing in some areas, while ignoring or under investing in others. For example, are you investing in your relationships? Are you investing in fun? Your portfolio will have its ups and downs, and Hot Spots allow you to identify areas that need the most attention. They can help you find key indicators for your personal performance. The portfolio metaphor helps you carve out time for what's important.

Balancing Your Hot Spots

Hot Spots give you a bit of scaffolding to help structure and support your life. When you have a set of Hot Spots, you can better balance your life. This works in conjunction with the portfolio metaphor. For example, are you investing the same time and energy in your work as in your personal life? Are you making time for fun? With the Hot Spots you have a frame for balancing your results.

Know Your Top 3 Pain Points and Opportunities

One way to achieve clarity of mind is to know your top three pain points and opportunities. In fact, the more you have going on in your life, the more you benefit from consolidating and organizing your pain and opportunities. This will help you focus when it counts. It will also help you avoid getting overwhelmed. It's also an easy way to turn pain and opportunity into action. The opposite is to have an endless list of pain points and an endless list of opportunities that you will never act on. Think of this as simply packaging up your pain and opportunities so that you can free up your mind and take action more effectively.

Organizing Your Hot Spots

At a high level, the simplest way to organize your Hot Spots is by three areas:

- Life Frame
- Work
- Personal

Life includes your key areas in life, such as your body, mind, or emotions. Work Hot Spots would include any projects, activities or roles at work. Personal Hot Spots would include any projects, activities or roles at home or anywhere outside of work.

Life Frame

This is the big picture. It's how you chunk up your overall time and energy. There are certain areas in life that if you invest in, you get rewarded. On the other hand, if you ignore these categories, you get penalized. Here's a starter set of categories you can use to think about the areas in your life that need your focus and energy:

Table 4.1 Life Frame

Hot Spots	Description
Mind	Includes investing time in learning thinking techniques and keeping your mind sharp.
Body	Includes investing time in keeping your body in shape and learning patterns and practices for health. The most important basics are eating, sleeping, and working out.
Emotions	Includes investing time in keeping your emotions healthy, learning emotional intelligence, and keeping your emotions in check. It's about learning skills for feeling good.
Career	Includes activities and projects for your job and other professional endeavors.
Financial	Includes investing time to learn patterns and practices for building and sustaining wealth.
Relationships	Includes your relationships at home, work, and life. The key is to create and maintain important, healthy relationships that add value to your life.
Fun	Includes investing time to play and do whatever you enjoy.

By identifying a set of Hot Spots, you can be more deliberate about how you spend your time and energy, as well as the trade-offs you make. You can also focus on finding key patterns and practices that help you improve in these areas.

Asking Questions with the Life Frame

You can use the Life Frame to help you ask better questions to drive results. Here are some example questions for each Hot Spot area:

Table 4.2 Asking Questions with the Life Frame

Hot Spots	Key Questions
Mind	How to improve your intellectual horsepower? How to improve critical thinking? How to ask better questions? How to find better answers to your questions?
Body	How to get fit? How to improve your body? How to manage your health?
Emotions	How to improve your emotional intelligence? How to feel good? How to deal with life's ups and downs?
Career	How to manage your career? How to climb the ladder? How to follow your passion?
Financial	How to build your wealth? How to protect your wealth? How to share your wealth?
Relationships	How to improve your relationships at work? How to improve your relationships at home? How to grow your network? How to leverage your network?
Fun	How to have fun? How to integrate fun into your life? How to balance play with work?

Setting Boundaries

You should set minimums and maximums for your Hot Spots in terms of time and energy. This keeps you from getting over-invested. Use your Hot Spots to set boundaries. For example, you might set a maximum on career and a minimum on relationships, body, and fun.

Table 4.3 Setting Boundaries with the Life Frame

Hot Spots	Boundaries
Mind	
Body	Minimum of 3 hours
Emotions	
Career	Maximum of 50 hours
Financial	
Relationships	Minimum of 8 hours
Fun	Minimum of 3 hours

In this case, step one is deciding to spend no more than 50 hours each week on your career Hot Spot. You're forced to bite off only what you can chew. This is how you start improving plate management and pushing back effectively. You can only spread your life force over so much. The categories help support each other. If not properly allocated, they can also work against each other.

Note that you might need to set the opposite limits. Set your limits and test results. The key is to use boundaries and limits to keep yourself balanced and improve your results. Schedule time in your calendar to reflect and reinforce these boundaries.

Key Insights

- When you set a minimum in the right categories, you avoid getting unbalanced and spending too much time or energy in a category at the expense of others.
- When you set a maximum in the right categories, you learn how to become more effective. For example, if you only have three hours to throw at a particular Hot Spot, you'll use them wisely.
- The worst mistake it to continually throw more time at problems.
- The key is to reduce time spent while increasing value and improving your efficiency and effectiveness.

Work Hot Spots

You can group your Hot Spots at work into the following buckets:
- Activities
- Active Projects
- Backlog

Work Hot Spots is a very simple way to get a handle on your job by thinking in terms of your recurring activities, any active projects that you're working on, and things that you plan to work on, but that you aren't actively working on right now (your backlog). By organizing your mind, you can improve your results and free up your mind to focus on higher-level strategies and outcomes.

To get a handle on your activities, identify your key activities, themes, and major roles and responsibilities. For example, you may have activities such as administration, managing budgets, mentoring, holding meetings, etc. Make a list for each big, recurring activity, role, or responsibility. This will let you see your job at a glance. You can then identify the main outcomes that you want for each of these activities. You may have a lot of outcomes or results that you want to achieve. In this case, list the most important three results at the top, and then list the rest after that. This way, you can quickly walk each significant activity, role or responsibility and see your three main outcomes at a glance.

For active projects, the first thing to do is make a list for each one of your active projects. This is your "queue." It's a place where you can queue up your work, rather than store it all in your head. This gives you a place to write down important outcomes or tasks. You can do the same for your backlog. Make one list for each project in your backlog that you are not actively working on. By having a list, you have a place to put things, rather than having them float around in your head. You know you have a good set of lists when you can quickly tell at a glance what all the current projects on your radar are. If you aren't used to thinking in terms of projects, simply think of all the balls you are currently juggling at work. In each project list, you should see a set of outcomes at a glance. The outcomes will help you see the forest from the trees.

The value of these lists is that they are a simple way to stay focused on what you want to accomplish. They are lightweight and scannable. They are easy to update or throw away as needed. They can help serve as scaffolding for your work life. By periodically reviewing these lists, you can very quickly remind yourself of what's important and you can very quickly adjust your plans if you're not getting where you want to go.

Personal Hot Spots

You can group your personal Hot Spots into the following buckets:
- Activities
- Active Projects
- Backlog

These are your personal projects or activities outside of work. This could be anything from writing a book to fixing the house. These are the balls you are juggling at home. And the advice just covered for work Hot Spots is applicable here as well.

Additional Considerations for the Life Frame Hot Spots

Your personal and work Hot Spots reflect your current projects and activities. Your Hot Spots create a simple, but effective map of "what's going on" in your life. Your life Hot Spots are a durable, but evolvable set of areas to invest in throughout your life. With this map in your hand, you can drill into any of the key areas of your work life or personal life or the bigger picture.

Sometimes when I explain the Life Frame to people, they want some elaboration on the Hot Spots. They want some of the next level down inside the buckets. Breaking the Hot Spots down into more actionable categories can help you get traction and make progress in that Hot Spot. For example, if I know I need to invest in "emotions" as a Hot Spot, how do I think about that? I can start by breaking emotions down into things like emotional intelligence, feeling good, passion, etc. Doing so can provide the clarity to define actionable steps. Next, I can look for and learn success patterns and good habits from books, mentors, or my own trial and error. It gives me way to focus my energy as well as organize any information or insight for that Hot Spot. You can imagine that over a lifetime, this creates a pretty deep personal knowledge base of insight and action.

The relationships Hot Spot is can also be a sticking point. People know that relationships are important, but they don't have an effective way to think about the various relationships in their life. Part of investing in your relationships means knowing how to map them out effectively. By having a simple way of looking at your relationships, you can more thoughtfully invest your time and energy in your relationships that really count. Your relationships serve as a foundation for the rest of your success, so it's worth adopting a new lens for looking at the people in your life.

In the next two sections, I share some examples of breaking Life Frame Hot Spots down into actionable categories, and how to think about the relationships Hot Spot in a way that's more actionable.

Examples of Life Frame Hot Spots

Here are some simple prompts to help you think of Hot Spots in your life. The list is not meant to be complete or exhaustive. You may want to add some other Hot Spots for your life, such as spiritual or social. The key is to have a simple heat map of what's important for you. It's a high level way to remind you to spread your life force across your meaningful buckets. It's a way to more thoughtfully invest in yourself.

Table 4.4 Example Hot Spots

Hot Spot	Example Hot Spots
Mind	• Anxiety (i.e., coping with and reducing anxiety) • Clarity (e.g., vision, purpose, task at hand, etc.) • Creativity • Critical Thinking • Learning • Mental Models • Optimism • Vision
Body	• Dental • Eating /Nutrition • Exercise (e.g., sports, weightlifting, Pilates, yoga, martial arts, etc.) • Health/Medical (e.g., disease, prevention, medicine, illness, hereditary or acquired diseases, etc.) • Senses (auditory, gustatory, kinesthetic, olfactory, and visual) • Sleeping • Stress • Systems (cardiovascular, digestive, endocrine, excretory, immune, skin, muscular, nervous, reproductive, respiratory, and skeletal)

Emotions	• Emotional Intelligence • Feeling Good (e.g., dealing with depression, loss, etc.) • Emotions (e.g., acceptance, anger, anticipation, disgust, fear, joy, sadness, surprise, etc.) • Empathy • Passion
Career	• Activities • Deliverables • Development • Expectations (e.g., yours, your boss's, etc.) • Outcomes • Projects • Relationships • Roles • Tasks
Financial	• Active Income • Budget • Business • Credit (e.g., debt, credit score, credit rating, etc.) • Insurance • Investments • Nest Egg • Passive Income • Retirement • Real Estate • Savings • Spending • Taxes
Relationships	• Family • Work • Circle of Friends
Fun	• Free Time • Hobbies/Interests • Indoor Recreation • Outdoor Recreation • Travel • Vacations

Relationships Hot Spot Explained

Investing in your relationships will serve you throughout your life. You can tell yourself you are a rock, you are an island, and you need no one, but the reality is you share the world with people, whether it's your family, your friends, the people at work, or the people in your community. Make the most of it.

Interactions and Roles

You can think of your relationships as the roles and interactions that are important in your life. More precisely, you can think of relationships as connections. You can then think of your roles in those connections. Your role is what part you play in that relationship. Your Hot Spots for relationships are any roles and interactions that are important in your life.

Table 4.5 Interactions and Roles

Hot Spots	Relationships	Roles
Family	Family, friends, relatives, etc.	Role model, grandparent, father, mother, sister, brother, etc.
Work	Teammates, peers, manager, partners, cross-team groups, key contacts, etc.	Manager, leader, mentor, etc.
Friends	Friends, community, groups, clubs, teams, special interest, online, etc.	Friend, neighbor, community leader, etc.

The idea in relationships is to invest based on what you want to accomplish. For example, be the father you want to be. Get the people on your side to make things easier at work or to sell your ideas. Be a great friend. Be a good role model. Be a great mentor.

Another important concept in relationships is to continuously invest. Life's not static. People will flow in and out of your life. Your relationships are growing, or they're dying.

In Summary

- Hot Spots are focal points and help you create a heat map of both opportunity and pain in your life.
- Know the three most important opportunities in your life.
- Know the three most important pain points in your life.
- Hot Spots as an investment portfolio helps you manage risk and determine where to invest your time for maximum results.
- By having a simple set of Hot Spots, you have a way to keep your life in check.
- Identity a simple set of Hot Spots for your life, your Life Frame (for example, mind, body, emotions, career, financial, relationships, and fun).
- Set boundaries for your time in your key Hot Spots (for example, a maximum of 40 – 50 hours in career, a minimum of 3 hours in body, a minimum of 8 hours in relationships).
- Schedule time in your calendar for your key Hot Spots.

Chapter 5 –
Monday Vision, Daily Outcomes, Friday Reflection

My future starts when I wake up every morning … Every day I find something creative to do with my life. —Miles Davis

In This Chapter
- Learn the Monday Vision, Daily Outcomes, Friday Reflection pattern for weekly results.
- Learn how to use Mondays to set your vision for a great week.
- Learn how to use The Rule of 3 for carving out daily results and weekly results.
- Learn how to use Fridays to reflect on your results and make improvements to your routine.

At the heart of Agile Results is the Monday Vision, Daily Outcomes, Friday Reflection pattern. It's a simple weekly pattern in which each week is a new chance to get results. On Mondays, you figure out three outcomes you want for the week. Each day, you determine your three most important outcomes. On Fridays, you reflect on your results. This pattern helps you tune and prune your results.

One of the most important techniques I share with those I mentor is how to manage their tasks. It's too easy to churn or find yourself in task saturation. Another common mistake is to confuse activities with outcomes. That is, you might spend a lot of time doing a lot of activities but not actually accomplish anything. In fact, I've seen many smart people throw a lot of hours at their weeks only to fail in one way or another. It might be that they ended up missing an important time window or losing any sort of work-life balance. In some cases, they spent all their time doing activities but not actually producing any results. In other cases, they produced results, only to find out it's not the results they needed or wanted.

How you frame and organize your results for the week plays an important part in your success. There are always more things to do than there is time in a day. It's easy to get overwhelmed. It's easy to beat yourself up over what you didn't finish. It's easy to spend all your time on task management. It's easy to find yourself at the end of the week, wondering where your time went. The reality is that without a system it's easy to get off track.

The solution is a system—a simple system you can count on, not have to think too hard to implement, and turn into a lifelong habit. In this system, each week is a fresh start. **If you fall off the horse, you can get back on.** Each week you know you're spending your time on the right things. Rather than feel overwhelmed by your backlog, you feel good about your accomplishments. Each week, you improve your ability to get results. That's the idea behind the Monday Vision, Daily Outcomes, Friday Reflection pattern.

Monday Vision, Daily Outcomes, Friday Reflection

Monday Vision, Daily Outcomes, Friday Reflection is a simple but effective pattern for results. It's time-tested. Here's the approach in a nutshell:

Table 5.1 Monday Vision, Daily Outcomes, Friday Reflection

Item	Description
Monday Vision	On Mondays, simply identify three outcomes—compelling results—you'd like for the week. If you've established what your Hot Spots are, use them for input.
Daily Outcomes	At the start of each day, identify three compelling outcomes you want to accomplish. Use your three outcomes for the week from your Monday Vision as input. You may have a laundry list of tasks, but for your Daily Outcomes, identify the three most important things you can accomplish for that day. You use these three outcomes to help you prioritize all of your tasks and focus on results. If you complete your three key outcomes for the day, you can always bite off more. Whenever you ask yourself what's the next best thing for you to do, your three outcomes should guide your answer.
Friday Reflection	Each Friday, make time to reflect on your results. This is your chance to see how you're doing at getting done what you set out to do. Identify three things that are going well. Identify three things that need improvement. This is a balanced look at your results. In addition, it's also a good time to check yourself against your three outcomes for the week and notice any recurring patterns.

That's the basic pattern. However, you can tailor it for your scenario. For example, maybe your week starts on a Sunday rather than on a Monday. What's important is those three parts. While the whole is more than the sum of its parts, each piece of the Monday Vision, Daily Outcomes, Friday Reflection pattern is significant. In fact, you can incrementally adopt each piece.

This is the same weekly pattern I've used for years to get results in extreme scenarios. It's helped me through the best of times—and the worst of times. It's the same pattern I've used to lead teams at Microsoft to ship on time and on budget while still keeping a work-life balance. It's the same system I've used to help the people I mentor get their life back and get on track. It works. What makes it work is that it's a simple way to organize your results. And it's self-correcting. What you learn each Friday, you can fold back into each new week.

Key Benefits

The Monday Vision, Daily Outcomes, Friday Reflection pattern provides a simple framework for you to organize each week. Here are the main benefits of adopting this pattern:

It's a Starting Point

It's a place to start. Even if your current approach is already working for you, you can improve it simply by adopting the routine of Monday Vision, Daily Outcomes, Friday Reflection.

It's Simple

It's simple enough that you can immediately apply it. On any given day, simply identify three outcomes for your day. If this is Monday, then identify three outcomes for your week. If this is Friday, reflect on your week and think of three things that went well and three things you'd like to improve. It really is that simple.

It Helps You Keep Your Eye on the Prize

Having three outcomes is a way to set yourself up for success. If you're accomplishing your results, then you know you're on the right track—good job! If you're not accomplishing your results, then you have to ask yourself whether you picked the right outcomes or if you need to improve your approach. As you practice each day, you get more effective.

It's an Easy Way to Stay on Track

Rather than ad hoc, it's a system. When you have a routine, you can improve it. If it's not working for you, you adjust it. It helps you get back on the saddle again.

It Helps You Make Course Corrections Sooner Rather than Later

It allows you to be more responsive to things that might arise.

It's just enough planning so that you have a map for your week, but you stay flexible. It's just-in-time so that your plans are timely and relevant. One of the worst pitfalls is to have a rigid system where you can't respond to change. Another common pitfall is to get bogged down in a system where the tool drives you. With this approach, you're the driver. You're in control. You always get to figure out what you're next best thing to do is in the context of the results you want to accomplish. Life can throw you curve balls. Having a weekly system for results helps you keep swinging at—and hitting—whatever life throws at you.

Why This Approach Works

Here's why this approach has worked for me and many others:
- It's self-correcting by providing opportunities for course corrections throughout the week as well as from week to week.
- You get rid of the noise in your head (the buzz of all the little MUSTs, SHOULDs, COULDs floating around).
- Unimportant items slough off. (Don't carry them forward—if they're important, you'll rehydrate them when needed.)
- You manage small and simple lists—never a big bloated list.
- It's not technology bound. When you're not at your desk, pen and paper work fine.

- Keeping your working set small helps you prioritize faster and make course corrections as needed.
- It's a system with simple habits and practices. It's a system to consistently check your path, allowing you to course-correct and integrate lessons learned.
- Your next actions—your MUSTs—are immediate and obvious relative to SHOULDs and COULDs.

Why some other approaches haven't worked:
- They were too complex or too weird.
- They ended up in monolithic lists or complicated slicing and dicing to get simple views for next actions.
- It was easy to get lost in activity instead of driving by outcome.
- They didn't account for the human side.
- Keeping the list (or lists) up-to-date and managing status were often more work than some of the actual to-do items.
- Stuff that should slough off wouldn't, and a snowball effect would ultimately make the approach unwieldy.

I've been using Agile Results now for years. I've tweaked and simplified it as I've shown others over time. While I learn every day, I particularly enjoy my Friday Reflections. I also found a new enjoyment in Mondays because I'm designing my days and driving my weeks.

Now that you have a better understanding of the strengths and benefits of the Monday Vision, Daily Outcomes, Friday Reflection pattern, let's take a closer look at how it works.

Monday Vision

Monday Vision is simply a practice where each Monday, you identify the most important outcomes for the week. This helps you work backwards with the results in mind. Knowing where you want to be by the end of the week, helps you stay focused during the week. It also helps you get in the habit of prioritizing your time and energy. There are a lot of things competing for your attention. This is your chance to draw a line in the sand and decide what you will and won't do.

3 Outcomes for the Week

Start with three outcomes. Simply identify three results for the week. Use questions to guide you. To do so, ask yourself questions such as, "If this were Friday, what are the three most important results I want to show?" and, "What would be the most pain if it weren't done by Friday?" Focus on outcomes, not activities or tasks. There's a good chance you may have lots of activities and tasks. This is about carving out three results for the week that you truly care about.

Daily Outcomes

Daily Outcomes are simply the three results you want for your day. This can be anything, such as completing a draft of a chapter in your new book, or having your best workout session, or finishing a meaningful slice of your project at work. You decide. Consider what you can reasonably accomplish and what would be the most valuable. Value is always in the eye of the beholder. Consider what's valuable for you, your family, your project, your team, your manager, etc.

3 Outcomes for Today

Identify your three best results for the day. That's it. You can always bite off more later. Challenge yourself to pick the three most valuable results that you can reasonably accomplish. This focus will help you quickly come to terms with prioritizing what's on your plate. You may have a sea of tasks. Don't get caught up in your backlog. Instead, think of the three most valuable things you can accomplish today and apply laser-like focus toward doing so. When you know that each move you make is working towards your meaningful outcomes, then you know that you're making your best plays given the circumstances. You can't control everything, but you can control your choices, your best moves, and your best responses for the situations you're in. Check your three outcomes for the day against your three outcomes for the week to see if you are on track and trending in the right direction.

MUST, SHOULD, COULD

There are lots of ways to rank and prioritize. For example, you might use numbering systems such as Priority 1, Priority 2, Priority 3 (or P1,

P2, P3). While this might be helpful in task management systems, I've found that in terms of a daily list, it helps to simply think in terms of MUST, SHOULD, and COULD. MUST is what you must get done, SHOULD would be nice, and COULD is just a pipe dream. There's something about the language that helps your brain prioritize better when you think in terms of MUST versus SHOULD or COULD. I've used numbering systems for my outcomes and to-dos in the past, but ultimately, I found better results, by using MUST, SHOULD, COULD to organize and prioritize my results. I've also found that many of the people I mentor had similar experiences. That said, if you prefer a numbering system, there's nothing stopping you from using a MUST, SHOULD, COULD mindset to help you organize your P1, P2, P3s.

Daily Outcomes Lists

You can use your Daily Outcomes as your to-do list. Each day, make a new list. Title it by date (for example, 2009-03-12). Start by listing your minimum MUST items, then your SHOULD and COULD items. Next, given your available time and energy, use The Rule of 3 to bubble up to the top of the list the three most compelling outcomes for you. Use this list throughout the day as you look through your various input streams for action. Your input streams include meetings, email, conversations, or bursts of brilliance throughout the day. Since you do this at the start of your day, you have a good sense of your priorities and can better deal with potentially randomizing scenarios. This list can also help you batch your work. For example, if you know there's a bunch of folks you need to talk to in your building, you might find that it would be more efficient to walk the halls rather than have email dialogues with them. On the other hand, if there are a lot of folks you need to email, you can batch that as well.

What's the Next Best Thing to Do?

When you find yourself wondering about your next steps, then first ask yourself, "What's the next best thing to do?" This simple question can go a long way. There may be things you want to do. There may be things that seem easy to do. While you may choose those for practical reasons, before doing so, answer whether that's the next best thing for you to do. At least then you know your trade-offs. If you need to get perspective, remind yourself of your three outcomes for the day and your three outcomes for the week.

Friday Reflection

Friday Reflection is a practice where you evaluate three things going well and three things to improve. By having a dedicated time for reflection, you can better focus on the "pitch" and not the "scoreboard" throughout the week. During the week, you perform; then on Friday, you evaluate. This helps you avoid over-analyzing yourself throughout the week. By focusing on both what's going well and what needs improvement, you also keep yourself balanced. It's all too easy to focus on just the negative and miss out on the positive—what's going well or what's working.

Friday Reflection is also a chance to evaluate what you got done—or didn't—and why. Because you have a flat list of to-do lists chunked up by day, it's very easy to review a week's worth and see patterns for improvement. It's actually easy for you to do this for months as well. Trends stand out. Analyzing is easy, particularly with continuous weekly practice. Your insight and key takeaways feed into your Monday Vision. Think of this as carrying forward the good, while letting go of the bad.

One way to make Friday Reflection a regular part of your weekly routine is to make it a recurring appointment on your calendar. For example, simply block off 30 minutes on Fridays at 10:00 a.m. You may not need the full time, but give yourself that time in case you need it. This is one of the most significant ways to continuously improve your quality of life, week over week. This is truly your chance to get clarity on your personal success patterns and what you need to change. It's also your chance to celebrate your wins and feel good about your ability to learn and respond.

Additional Considerations

Here are some additional considerations to keep in mind and help you when you adopt the Monday Vision, Daily Outcomes, Friday Reflection pattern.

1. **Value Delivered over Backlog Burndown.** Rather than just focus on reducing your backlog, think in terms of flowing value. This will impact both your mindset and your results. Rather than feel like a slave to a backlog, you'll be making conscious decisions

over what your next best thing to do is, whether it's an item from your existing backlog, or capitalizing on a new opportunity. This is agility in action.

2. **The Rule of 3.** Whenever you feel overwhelmed, turn to The Rule of 3. Set simple limits. You may have hundreds of tasks in your backlog, but take the time to figure out your three most meaningful results for today. This will give you clarity, focus, and peace of mind. When you know you're working on the right things, it's easy to stay fully engaged and produce your best results.

3. **Framing Results for the Week.** Framing your results is simply how you picture it in your mind, or how you help others picture what your results will look like. The more you practice framing your results for the week (by getting a good vision of what your three results will really look like), the easier it gets. Clarity is a skill.

4. **Tests for Success.** Identify and define your own tests for success. You get to define three outcomes for the day and the week. Imagine in your mind what success looks like. If achieving the results won't actually be a success, then you need to either redefine success or redefine your outcomes. This is a great way to practice setting and resetting expectations both for yourself and others.

5. **Scenario-Driven Results.** A good way to figure out tests for success is to use scenarios or to craft stories. For example, if you're working on your backyard, walk the scenarios that matter to you. You might prioritize having a barbeque on your deck, laying in your hammock and enjoying your rose garden as key scenarios to optimize around. Rather than just mow the lawn or clean up the back, now you have specific scenarios or experiences that you are lighting up and making happen. This gives your work meaning, and it improves the quality of your life, simply by focusing and concentrating your effort toward your next best things to do.

6. **Find a Way to Flow Value.** You can always make incremental progress. Remember that value is in the eye of the beholder. If you aren't flowing value, either to yourself or to others, then something is off. See if you can chunk your results down. One way to do this is to have a "show and tell" where you show your results to others. Your show and tell could be demonstrating some software you built, or it could be as simple as showing off a room in your house that you cleaned. If people don't value what you are showing, you'll know earlier rather than later, and you can adjust your approach.

7. **Have a Buffer.** Life happens. No matter how well you plan or how predictable things seem, things sometimes suddenly come up. Have a buffer for them. Bite off what you can without having a plate that's so full that you're paranoid about running into your boss and getting yet another item to add on top. You also don't want to be in the situation where one more straw breaks the camel's back. Think of your work like a buffet: instead of piling it on, take smaller portions, clear your plate faster, and make multiple trips. This will keep you lighter, more agile, and more responsive to any opportunities. If you're plate is too full and you have no buffers, you won't see any opportunities—only threats to your already over-burdened schedule.

8. **Timeboxes.** Use time limits to help you spend your energy more effectively, and to invest your time across the things that matter most. A timebox is simply a limit or constraint in terms of how much time you will spend on something. This helps you avoid overspending your time in one area at the expense of another.

In Summary

- The Monday Vision, Daily Outcomes, Friday Reflection pattern helps you make the most of each week. On Mondays, figure out three results for the week. Each day, decide on three outcomes for the day. On Fridays, ask yourself what three things are going well and what three things need improvement. Reflect on your results.
- It's a flexible, adaptable system that you can tailor to suit your needs.
- Because it's a system, you can tune and prune it based on what you learn about yourself and the situation or context that you find yourself in.
- Focus on outcomes. Your outcomes should sound like results or achievements, not activities and tasks.
- Use the system to support you in whatever you need, whether it's personal results at home or personal results on the job. Trust the system as a way to help you see the forest from the trees while dealing with your everyday tasks and activities.

Part II – Daily, Weekly, Monthly, Yearly Results

In This Part:

- Chapter 6 – Design Your Day
- Chapter 7 – Design Your Week
- Chapter 8 – Design Your Month
- Chapter 9 – Design Your Year

Chapter 6 – Design Your Day

It's not the daily increase but daily decrease. Hack away at the unessential. —Bruce Lee

In This Chapter

- Learn how to set yourself up for success each day using "tests for success."
- Learn how to structure your day to maximize your results.
- Learn how to chunk your day to avoid being overwhelmed.

Is your day by design or by default? One of the simplest ways to improve your day is to use The Rule of 3 to identify three results you want for the day. When you know what you want to accomplish, you can work backwards from that. Another way to improve your day is to add more power hours. It's not how much time you have; it's how you spend it. You can choose to spend your power hours having fun, blasting through obstacles, or achieving important results in your life. If you think of your day as a fixed budget of time, you can carve out time for what's important. For example, have you made time for free time? Have you made time to invest in the important Hot Spots in your life (mind, body, emotions, career, financial, relationships, and fun)? The secret of a successful day is enjoying your startup routine, spending your time on compelling outcomes, enjoying the process, making time for what's important (including free time), and ending your day in a way that supports you.

Each day is a fresh start. Remember as a kid waking up each morning to a new and exciting day? That's the point you need to start from. The difference is now you have skills. You also picked up some good habits and some bad habits. You looked forward to growing up so you could do whatever you want. Unfortunately over time, maybe you started to think that life isn't as full of possibilities or as limitless as you once thought. But what's limiting you? You are, and all the limits you bring to each new day. Baggage brings you down. Don't pick up your bags today. Travel light. Test yourself. Test your limits. Chances are you'll surprise yourself time and again; just give yourself a chance. If things don't work out today, then you can still walk away with lessons that will help you shape a better tomorrow.

Given that we spend our lives one day at a time, the real difference in our lives is how we spend each day. We're creatures of habit, and it's easy to fall into habits or routines that limit us. While you won't get more time each day, you can choose how you spend it. You can think about your day in terms of activities. Or, you can think about your day in terms of events or highlights. You can also use outcomes or results as a gauge for your day. It really boils down to what you spend your time on, the quality of how you spend it, and who you spend your time with.

Designing Your Day

You can structure your day for success. The following table summarizes how to map out your day using key practices:

Table 6.1 Designing Your Day

Item	Key Practices
Start Your Day	• Start with The Rule of 3 • Startup Routine
Design Your Day	• Scan Your Hot Spots • Compelling Outcomes • Scenario-Driven Results • Carve Out Time for What's Important • Set Boundaries and Limits
Drive Your Day	• Wear the Right Hat • Worst Things First • Pace Yourself • Power Hours • Test Your Results
End Your Workday	• Dump Your State • Hang Your Hat Up
End Your Day	• 4 Questions to Cap Your Day • Shutdown Routine

Now, we'll walk through these key practices so that you know what to do for each one.

Start Your Day

A good startup routine helps set the pace for the rest of your day. If you wake up and want to immediately crawl back to bed, that's not an effective start. It's not, however, necessarily about starting your day bright-eyed and bushy-tailed with sunshine, blue skies, and a bluebird on your shoulder. It's about starting the day on your terms in a way that empowers you to be your best.

Start with The Rule of 3

If you remember nothing else, start your day with The Rule of 3. Know the minimum you want for the day—simply identify three results. These are your "tests for success." It's your chance to define your success, and you get a clean slate each day.

Here are some of the main reasons to start your day with The Rule of 3:

- You define the three tests for success. If you set the rules, you win the game.
- You get to define what good looks like.
- You get to chart your course. If you start by quickly looking over the time you'll spend for the day, then you have a map to guide you through your day and to lead you if you get lost in the thick of things.
- If you know what you're trying to accomplish, you can prioritize more effectively. There are a lot of little mini-decisions during your day that you can influence by knowing where you want to go.
- If you know you're working on the right things, it's easier to give your all—to find your motivation.
- When you map your day, you know how to pace yourself. You can't run ahead if you can't see what's in front of you.

Remember that your three outcomes aren't tasks. You might have lots of tasks that roll up to these three outcomes, but these are three results you want for the day. For example, for today I want a draft of my chapter complete, a fun lunch, and a strawman of my project plan. Those are the lines I've drawn in the sand for the day.

Startup Routine

This is how you bootstrap your day. You already have a startup routine. It's the activities you do to start your day and feel grounded. For example, on weekdays, my startup routine is to wake up, workout for 30 minutes, shower, eat breakfast slowly, and take the back way to work. On my drive to work, I listen to my favorite music, and I think of my three most compelling outcomes for the day. When I get to work, I scan my inbox, my queues, and my calendar to see if I need to adjust my three outcomes.

Design Your Day

Designing your day is a simple exercise in creating enough scaffolding for your day. It helps you keep track of your day so it doesn't get away from you. It also reminds you of what's important and steers you clear from spending time on things that don't move you closer to where you want to be. Designing your day is as easy as deciding three outcomes you want and then spending the day thinking, feeling, and doing whatever it takes to accomplish that. If you accomplish your three outcomes, you can always bite off more. You can also adjust your three outcomes if you find they just aren't the right things for right now. What's important is that you first explicitly define what you want to accomplish.

Scan Your Hot Spots

Think of your Hot Spots as a heat map of what's important. At a high level, you have a stable set of Hot Spots for life: mind, body, emotions, career, financial, relationships, and fun. By investing in these areas throughout your life, you set yourself up for success. You also have Hot Spots for work, such as your active projects and any important roles or activities or events. You also have Hot Spots for your personal projects and roles, whether that's fixing up your house, going on an adventure, or being a parent.

You should have a map of your Hot Spots in easy view, whether you write them on paper or store them electronically. The point is this—at a glance, you can quickly see all the balls you are juggling, and you can use the Hot Spots as a way to cherry-pick what the most important value is that you can deliver (whether to yourself or to others). It boils down to reducing pain and increasing pleasure. Some of your Hot Spots will represent opportunities in your life, while other Hot Spots will represent the leaks in your life that you need to fix. While it's easy to get in the habit of only working on the most painful Hot Spots, stop and think whether you need to start investing more of your time and energy in Hot Spots that really change your game and open new doors. Don't get stuck simply treading water and reducing pain. Strike a balance. Carve out a chunk of your life force for working on improvements and leading the life you want to live.

Compelling Outcomes

Turn your heat map into compelling outcomes. If Hot Spots are the areas that need your time and energy, outcomes are the results you want. After you scan your Hot Spots, boil them down into a set of results or outcomes you would like to see. Keep it simple. It's counter-productive to make a laundry list of results you want. This is about distilling a few good enough results for now that you can reasonably make progress on. One way to figure this out is to identify what results you want for the week. If you know what you want for the week, then you can back it up from there to determine the results you need for today to get closer to where you want to be. If that's not big picture enough, then think about the three results you want for the month, or even the year. The point is to make it compelling. If you have a compelling "Why," you'll find a way.

No matter what task or activity you work on, you can also identify compelling outcomes. It's one thing to work on a task. It's another to know what the outcomes are and what good looks like. You can identify tests for success that inspire you along the way. If this is a task you're doing for yourself, you can identify your own tests for success. If this is a task you're doing for somebody else, why not ask them what good looks like? Involve them. This way you don't get surprised when you finish and they aren't impressed. You can help reduce crossed expectations.

Scenario-Driven Results

Walk the scenarios. This is a way to test what good might look like. For example, rather than a laundry list of tasks (such as mow the lawn, clear the bushes, rake the leaves, etc.), turn it into a scenario, such as "enjoy the yard." Then you can evaluate whether mowing the lawn is the next best thing to do. Perhaps the lawn is OK for now, but if you trimmed the tree so that you can use the hammock ... now, that would really make it a great experience. Simply by visualizing the scenario or the experience you want, you get an idea of what you're working towards. It's a quick and simple exercise that helps you find your way through the laundry list of chores. It's also the same technique that helps you find compelling outcomes. Simply by turning all your activities into compelling outcomes and using scenarios and experiences to test the end in mind, you dramatically improve your ability to get results.

Carve Out Time for What's Important

You don't have time, you *make* time. If you don't make time for what's important, it doesn't happen. This is where The Rule of 3 helps. Are you spending the right amount of time today on those three results you want to accomplish? The default pattern is to try and fit them in with all your existing routines. A more powerful approach is to make time for your three results today and optimize around that. This might mean disrupting other habits and routines you have, but this is a good thing. **The more you get in the habit of making time for what's important, the more you'll get great results.** If you're not getting the results you want, you can start asking better questions. For example, are you investing enough time? Are you investing the right energy? Are you using the right approach? Or, maybe a different thing happens. Maybe you start accomplishing your results but don't like what you get. You can step back and ask whether you're choosing the right outcomes for The Rule of 3.

Here are some things to think about when you're carving out your time:

- *How much time minimum should you spend today for each of your three outcomes?*
- *How much time maximum should you spend today for each of your three outcomes?*

- Are you spending too much energy in below the line activities? (This is where you're just treading water and making it through each day, but not actually getting ahead.)
- Are you spending enough time in above the line activities? (This is where you feel you're on top of your day and investing your time where you get the most impact.)
- Are you investing time in the most important Hot Spots in your life: mind, body, emotions, career, financial, relationships, fun?

Set Boundaries and Limits

Chunking up your day is easier if you use timeboxes and set boundaries. You can set boundaries at a high level. For example, you might decide that breakfast is at 8:00 a.m., lunch is at 12:00 noon, and dinner is at 5:30 p.m. In addition, you might decide that your workout is from 7:00 a.m. to 8:00 a.m. and that nothing gets in the way. Lastly, you might also decide that you'll take "weekends off" but work intensely during the week. What's important is that you do this by design and not by default. If you just do the default it can be easy to spend all your time in the wrong places or spend too much time in one area at the expense of another.

One of the most important things you can do is to fix time for eating, sleeping and working out. If you fix time for these three things and then work your day around these, you help set yourself up for success. Think of these as part of your personal success patterns and fine tune them. For example, look back through your life and decide, what was the most effective approach you had for working out? What were your best routines for eating and sleeping? If you don't have routines that work, now you know to prioritize and figure them out.

You can also set up boundaries and limits for accomplishing your three outcomes for the day. Decide on the minimum and maximum time you want to allocate for each. It's answering the question, "What's the range of time and energy you want to spend to make it happen?" This helps you avoid over-investing or even under-investing. It's also easy to underestimate the amount of work involved. If each day what you estimate to take three hours takes you six hours instead, then you need to pay attention. This is your chance to start practicing how you estimate your time. You'll get better with practice.

Drive Your Day

Drive or be driven. It's easy to spend your day reacting, especially if you don't have a plan. Once you have a plan, you at least have a rough map for your day. You still need to be flexible, but at least you've charted a potential course. Now that you have a map, it's easy to decide on things such as whether you can take a leisurely stroll or whether you need to get it in gear and really kick some arse. Driving your day is the thinking, feeling, and doing part. It's the execution of your results. If you start your day with three outcomes you want to accomplish, then you can drive your day. If you're not driving, you're reacting.

Wear the Right Hat

Adopt the right mindset for the situation. Using a hat as a metaphor, you can wear different hats for different situations. For example, maybe you need a more exploratory mindset, so you put on your explorer's cap. Maybe you need to kick some arse and take names; that's another hat. Either way, this is about recognizing that your mindset will be the biggest influence on how you approach your day and how you react to it. Switch out hats that aren't working. Have a set of hats you can trust and wear the right hat for the job.

Worst Things First

This is a practice I learned long ago—doing worst things first. It's human nature to move away from pain. But rather than save your biggest hurdle for the end, do it up front when you are your strongest. The idea is to "get it over with." For instance, sometimes I have a meeting or a conversation or even just a task for the day that I'm not looking forward to. I'm not talking about the stuff I can ignore forever. I'm talking about the stuff that needs to happen sooner rather than later, but that I won't enjoy doing. Whenever possible, I try to schedule these hurdles for the earlier part of my day or week when I'm at my strongest. Don't let things loom over you. If you push those things to the end of the day or the end of the week, they loom. Why loom longer than necessary? That's draining. One of my mentors gave me this tip, worst things first, and it has become one of my most effective habits.

Power Hours

Having power hours is your best asset for the day. A power hour is when you feel at your strongest and in the zone. You accomplish more in that one power hour than you do spending several hours or even days not in the zone.

If you don't have a single power hour in your day (or just don't know when it is), then it's job one to find it. Look back on your day and your week to answer these questions:

- *Are there times that you seem to get a whole lot done no matter what the task?*
- *Do you find you concentrate better at certain times of the day?*
- *When do you feel like a fully fueled race car rather than a broken-down jalopy?*

At first, you might find yourself with only one or two power hours a day. As you pay attention to your power hours, you can start to find ways to have more power hours in your day. For example, if you find that just taking a quick, five minute walk gets the creative juices flowing again, then you've found a way to create a power hour on demand. You can spend your power hours on whatever you want. The key is to set yourself up to have power hours in the first place.

Pace Yourself

When you have a map of your results, it's easier to set your pace. If you only have one speed, then you're not enjoying the spectrum or cycles of your day. Rather than think of it as a marathon, think of the day as a series of sprints. When you take your breaks, really take your breaks. When you're working, be fully engaged. Don't spend all your time doing everything halfway. It's not engaging, and you won't find your flow. Give your best where you have your best to give and maximize your energy bursts. Make the most of them and set yourself up for more. Just like any muscle, your energy reserves get stronger as you flex them.

Test Your Results

Testing your results is one of the most important practices you can adopt. First, it's thinking about how you can break your own limits and surprise yourself. Second, you want to test your assumptions about the work as early as possible and find any surprises. Really, this is about both exploring your limits and testing ideas against reality. The quicker you test your results, the quicker you get feedback to make better decisions as well as find any fallback plans if needed.

Rather than decide up front whether you can do this or you can't do that or that's impossible, start testing your results and inform your own opinion. It's easy to let your past failures limit your future successes. But keep in mind that scenarios can make a big difference; so does your approach. If you've failed before, it may have very well been due to the scenario, the context, or your approach. In that case, learn what you can from the experience but don't let it get in the way of your future results.

End Your Workday

When you end your workday, the last thing you want is for your wheels to keep spinning. Here are a few practices that you can use to help you transition from work.

Dump Your State

Some of the most effective people I know use this simple practice—they dump their state at the end of the day. They write down whatever they were working on so that they can easily pick up where they left off. Whether this is in a notebook or a text file, what's important is that it's in a place you trust.

Hang Your Hat Up

Just going home doesn't cut it. You need a transition. You need to shift your mind from thoughts of work to thoughts of home. One practice some people use is to hang their hat up. They simply visualize a tree in front of their house, and they hang their hat up on that tree before they go inside. They can then pick their hat up the next day. Another approach you can use is to start asking yourself different questions that aren't work-related, such as, "What would I like to do tonight for fun?" Changing the questions changes your focus.

End Your Day

How you end your day matters. Simply by adding certain routines, you can improve your day's end and set yourself up for success. One routine is to ask yourself four questions to help put the focus on some of the most important aspects of your day. The other is to have an effective shutdown routine. Both routines help you wind down from your day.

4 Questions to Cap Your Day

At the end of each day, I ask myself the following:

1. *What did I learn?*
2. *What did I improve?*
3. *What did I enjoy?*
4. *What kind act did I do?*

I use these questions to reflect on daily improvements as well as course-correct. I also use them to appreciate life's little lessons each day. It's a simple practice, but it helps make sure I don't slip into life's auto-pilot mode. What's interesting too is that this simple practice can actually raise your happiness level by focusing on important aspects of your day in a positive light.

Shutdown Routine

This is how you end your day. Just like having an effective startup routine helps bootstrap your day, an effective shutdown routine helps you wind down. The key to an effective shutdown routine is testing different patterns until you find one that helps put you in the right frame of mind for a more restful sleep. Sleeping well is the means to starting the next day refreshed.

You might think it would be easy enough to think of a great shutdown routine, but there are a lot of variables. It's actually better to test a variety of patterns to see what helps you the most, whether it's watching TV, reading a book, meditating, etc. For example, if you tend to watch the news before you sleep, test watching a comedy; different shows will produce different results. If you like to read a book before bed, are you reading a book that helps you wind down, or are you reading material that makes it hard for you to fall asleep? Simply notice the results you're getting and test different approaches.

There's a lot of research and opinions, but the most important thing is to find what works for you. It's less about the activity you do and more about how it impacts you or how you react to it. For example, if you watch a comedy where the main character always gets into a stressful situation, and you have a lot of empathy, maybe this is not the best thing for you before bed. Then again, maybe the happy ending is just the perfect tension and release you need for the perfect slumber. Test your results and change your approach if it's not working. At the end of the day, you're the most important judge.

Lastly, in addition to how you feel at the end of your day, it's also important to notice how you feel when you wake up. If you're not waking up refreshed, chances are that it's what you did the night before that makes all the difference (barring any medical conditions, of course). So go ahead and find what works for you. Test some new patterns. Get creative. Explore your results.

Example of a Day by Design

Here's an example of a day by design:

Table 6.2 Example of a Day by Design

Item	Examples
Outcomes	3 outcomes • Finish my review (must/don't want) • Email to team for new path (should) • Mock up a new design (should/want) To-dos • Clear inbox • Catch up with Jason • Research effective user experience patterns • Synch with Bob on the approach
Startup	7:00 – 8:30 a.m.—Workout, shower, and breakfast

Administration	9:00 – 9:30 a.m.—Clear mail, check calendar, and prioritize.
	4:00 – 4:30 p.m.—Clear mail
Think Time	8:30 – 9:00 a.m.—Drive to work
	9:30 – 10:00 a.m.
Power Hours	10:00 – 11:00 a.m.
	1:00 – 2:00 p.m.
	3:00 – 4:00 p.m.
Breaks	12:00 – 1:00 p.m.—Lunch
	2:00 – 2:30 p.m.
	6:00 – 7:00 p.m.—Dinner
Play Time	5:00 – 6:00 p.m.
	8:00 – 9:00 p.m.
Shutdown	10:00 p.m.—4 Questions to Cap Your Day
	10:30 – 11:00 p.m.—Read
	11:00 p.m.—Sleep

Additional Considerations

The following are some additional considerations for improving your day:

Action Before Motivation

Stop waiting for lightning to strike. Just start; don't wait for inspiration to come. Can you imagine if athletes only trained when they were inspired? This will seem especially counter-intuitive if you're the type that waits for inspiration. The truth, however, is that some days you will get inspiration, and other days you won't. That's the nature of the beast. The key though is that you raise your chances for inspiration by getting up to bat. In many cases, you'll find that while you don't start off inspired, once you take action, your motivation follows. For instance, you may have an exercise routine that you aren't inspired to do, but once you're doing it, you may find you actually enjoy it (or at the very least, find enough motivation to keep going). If you're saying to yourself, "I don't feel like doing it," remind yourself that you might feel like doing it once you're actually doing it.

Execution Checklists

Creating execution checklists is a simple, but effective technique for improving results. An execution checklist is not a to-do list. It's a list of steps in sequence to perform a specific task. To create it, I simply write the main steps down before I start the task. This helps me plan the main steps while I'm in think-mode. Then, while I'm running through the steps, I don't have to think too hard about what to do next or get lost in the steps. There are two main scenarios:

1. **You are planning the work to be executed.** In this case, you're thinking through what you have to get done. This is great when you feel over-burdened or if you have a mind-numbing, routine task that you need to get done. This can help you avoid task saturation and reduce silly mistakes while you're in execution mode.

2. **You are paving a path through the execution.** In this case, you're leaving a trail of what worked. This works great for tasks that you'll have to perform more than once or you have a routine you want to improve.

I encourage you to create execution checklists for any friction points or sticking spots you hit. For example, if there's a routine you have with lots of movable parts, capture the steps down and tune them over time as you gain proficiency. As simple as this sounds, it's very effective whether it's for a personal task, a team task, or any execution steps you want to improve.

Worry Breaks

In his book, *Shed 10 Years in 10 Weeks*, Dr. Julian Whitaker suggests taking a "worry break." If you find yourself stressed with worry throughout the day, then consolidate it. Designate a half-hour break for worrying; it's better than randomly entertaining these thoughts throughout the day. During your break, worry as much as you want and as intensely as you want. Let yourself think of all the worst-case scenarios. By having a designated time for this, you make it easier to stay focused during the rest of your day. When you start to worry, remind yourself that you made a specific time for it. The more you stick to using your worry breaks, the less distracted you'll get throughout your day.

Another benefit of consolidating you worries into a worry break is that you give your troubles their own focus so that you can begin to address them and start to find more effective patterns. For example, you may find that some of your problems can be broken down into smaller problems and tackled as needed. While in other cases, seeing a group of problems together may lead you to discover a common solution. Then there are other worries that just needed a moment of your time, but now it's time to let go.

Creative Hours

Creative hours are those times when your mind feels free to explore ideas: creating new ideas from scratch, putting new ideas together, or simply reflecting. They're really a state of mind—a state of daydreaming. It's the mindset that's important. Whereas your power hours may be focused on results, your creative hours are focused on free-form thinking and exploration. You might find that creative hours are your perfect balance to power hours. You might also find that you thrive best when you add more creative hours to your week. Ultimately, you might find that your power hours free up time for your creative hours, or that your creative hours change the game and improve your power hours. Your power hours might also be how you leverage your ideas from your creative hours. Test your results.

Make It Work, Then Make It Right

This is a simple rule of thumb that can help you dramatically accomplish more. Rather than try to perfect things as you go along, try to complete things first. Then go back and improve them. If you try to improve as you go, you often won't know when to stop. Worse, you won't complete things. If you don't complete things, all your improvements along the way are insignificant because you never get to the point where you or anybody else can enjoy them. On the other hand, if you bite off enough to complete a meaningful chunk and make it work, then you can show off what you've accomplished so far while deciding how "right" you want to make it. This builds momentum. Always find the simplest path through to get to a working result. Then go back and improve as needed. By having working results, you'll build your confidence and momentum. More people fail by never finishing or by wallowing in perfectionism or analysis paralysis. Your chances are better by getting working results you can improve. Make it work, and then make it right.

Batch and Focus

Consolidate similar tasks and do them in a batch. This helps you reduce task switching and improve your efficiency. If you have to keep task switching, changing focus, and hopping around, you'll break your rhythm and you won't get the benefit of batching.

Test Drive Your Results

Get in the habit of doing dry runs. If you're in the habit of thinking everything through in your head, shift to thinking less and doing more. You'll find that there are many things you can't anticipate. Instead, of focusing on anticipating, focus on learning and responding. Take action, learn, and respond. This will help keep you out of analysis paralysis. More importantly, you'll produce more effective results. You'll also find your surprises earlier versus later. Testing your results helps you very quickly find gaps, surprises, or dependencies so you can adapt as needed before you paint yourself into a corner.

Reduce Friction

Find ways to reduce friction. Friction can be anything from a sloppy desk to an over-complicated task you need to perform regularly. Friction adds up and can eventually provide enough resistance that you stop doing the activity entirely, often to your own detriment. Create glide paths so that you can more easily fall into the right habits and practices. For example, leave your sneakers by your bed so you can just get up and run first thing in the morning, or put your favorite music within easy reach of your workout. I routinely do a quick sweep of my desk before I start work. I spend no more than 10 minutes. Doing so allows me to carve out a nice clean space free of distractions, and I can get to work with nothing in my way.

Quantify It

Sometimes setting a quota is better than using a timebox. For example, can you think of three compelling goals for your year? Can you think of three results for today that you would enjoy working on?

When you get stuck on something that seems large and overwhelming, then try chunking it down into smaller quantities. Start with a number you can easily hit and then add more. Can you do one push up? OK, now let's go for three. The key is to think in terms of incremental hurdles. This will help you deal with problems that overwhelm you as well as with information overload. Eat an elephant a bite at a time.

In Summary

- Structure you day for success. Begin by creating three compelling outcomes. Scan your Hot Spots.
- Create a startup routine.
- Create compelling outcomes.
- Carve out time for what's important.
- Create a shutdown routine.

Chapter 7 – Design Your Week

A goal is not always meant to be reached; it often serves simply as something to aim at. —Bruce Lee

In This Chapter

- Learn how to design a week for sustainable results.
- Learn how to add more power hours to your week.
- Learn how to make more free time each week.

You can use the Monday Vision, Daily Outcomes, Friday Reflection pattern for weekly results. This simple pattern gives you a fresh start each week and each day. Using The Rule of 3, you can bite off three things for the week and three things each day. By designing your week, you can spend more time in your strengths and less time in your weaknesses. This will improve your energy and help you continuously renew. The most important thing you can do is fix time for core activities that keep you going: eating, sleeping, and working out. Investing in these is investing in yourself.

Is your week by design or by default? **One of the keys to results is owning your schedule.** You can drive your schedule, or it can drive you. Imagine a week where you spend each day working on the right things with the right people and making the right impact. Imagine looking forward to the start of the week, whether it's because it's a fresh start, or it's a chance to experience more of what you want. Imagine spending more time each day on the things that make you strong, give you energy and make you feel powerful. Imagine a week filled with power hours, creative think time, and enough free time that you feel balanced and effective. Imagine a week where you get enough sleep, get enough movement, and have enough energy to accomplish whatever you want. This is a week by design. It's not just about weekly results; it's about sustainable results.

Your week is a large chunk of time to get a handle on. By designing a week that supports you, you set yourself up for weekly results. Each week is a fresh start. You can carry the lessons forward from one week into the next. All you really have is time, so the key is to make the most of it. If you have recurring activities, you probably added them over time without realizing it; that's a schedule by default, not by design. **Seize the opportunity now to design a week which actually supports you.**

Designing Your Week

Table 7.1 Designing Your Week

Item	Key Practices
Map Out Your Week	• Baseline Your Schedule • Identify Committed Time • Map Out Your Strengths and Weaknesses • Identify Free Time
Design Your Week	• Set Boundaries and Limits • Fix Time for Eating, Sleeping, and Working Out • Carve Out Time for What's Important • Consolidate Related Activities • Consolidate Weaknesses • Add Strengths • Schedule Free Time
Drive Your Week	• Scan Your Hot Spots • Start with The Rule of 3 • Monday Vision, Daily Outcomes, Friday Reflection
End Your Week	• Friday Reflection • Show-and-Tell

Map Out Your Week

Before you can improve your week, you first need a bird's-eye view of your schedule; creating a simple map of your week helps. If you know what your week looks like at a glance, it's easier to spot problems. It's also easier to test potential solutions in terms of rearranging your schedule. Having a simple map of your week makes it easy to play with "What if" scenarios, such as, what if I used Monday to take care of most of my administrative tasks or what if I used Friday to catch up with people.

Baseline Your Schedule

Start by mapping out your week and get a good baseline of your schedule. To create a map, you can create a simple matrix. Include the hours and the days of the week. Here's an example template:

Table 7.2 Baseline Your Schedule

	Sun	Mon	Tue	Wed	Thu	Fri	Sat
7:00 a.m.							
8:00							
9:00							
10:00							
11:00							
12:00							
1:00 p.m.							
2:00							
3:00							
4:00							
5:00							
6:00							
7:00							
8:00							
9:00							
10:00							

On your map, write down your activities and how you spend your time. Here are some key things to include:
*   Sleeping
*   Eating
*   Workouts
*   Meetings

- Work time
- Free time
- Activities

Identify Committed Time

Identify your committed time. These are scheduled items that aren't flexible. This might include meetings, other people's schedules, or activities that you can't move. Your goal is simply to map out which time is fixed versus which time is flexible.

Identify Free Time

Identify your free time. It might be scattered all over the board. You might find you don't even have any free time. Your goal is simply to map out what your current free time is. Be honest. You'll get a chance to fix it. What's important is that you take a good look at what it currently is.

Map Out Your Strengths and Weaknesses

Identify which activities make you weak and which activities make you strong. If you're not sure, start by thinking about which activities you look forward to and which activities you dread. The goal is to be able to see your activities at a glance and know whether they make you weak or strong.

Design Your Week

By shuffling your schedule around, you can make some dramatic improvements in your energy and how you feel. It's not about making a perfect week. It's about making improvements in how you spend your time. Here are the keys to designing your week:

- First baseline your schedule. Note your committed time and free time.
- Consolidate activities that make you weak as much as possible.
- Move those activities that make you weak to the morning when you can.
- Spend more of your time on your strengths.
- Create time blocks to consolidate, batch and focus on key activities.

- Make time for important activities, including alone time, fun time, time with people, etc.
- Push for spending 75 percent of your time each day in activities that make you strong. Push the 25 percent of the time you spend in weaknesses, to the start of your day. Think of this as worst things first. By getting your weaknesses out of the way, you can spend the rest of your day in your strengths. Another way to do this is to push the main things that make you weak to the start of your week. Eliminating them early creates a glide path for the rest of the week.

Set boundaries and limits

Setting boundaries and limits is how you achieve your balance. If you don't make time for things, they won't happen. If you don't set limits for things, they will take over other important parts of your life. Start with simple boundaries; here are some examples:

- Dinner on the table at 5:30 p.m.
- No work on the weekend.
- Tuesday night is date night.

Try using Hot Spots and setting boundaries. Set a maximum on career and a minimum on relationships, body, and fun. Here's an example:

Table 7.2 Set Boundaries and Limits

Hot Spot	Minimums and Maximums (per week)
Mind	
Body	Minimum of 3 hours
Emotions	
Career	Maximum of 50 hours
Financial	
Relationships	Minimum of 8 hours
Fun	Minimum of 3 hours

Don't spread your life force too thinly. The Hot Spots categories support each other.

Key Insights

- When you set a minimum in the right categories, you avoid getting unbalanced and improving other categories.
- When you set a maximum in the right categories, you learn how to become more effective. For example, if you only have eight hours to throw at your day, you'll use them wisely.
- The worst mistake is to throw more time at problems. The key is to reduce time spent, while increasing value and improving effectiveness and efficiency.

The first step is to decide to spend no more than 50 hours each week on work. This forces you to bite off only what you can chew. This is how you start improving time management and pushing back effectively.

Fix Time for Eating, Sleeping, and Working Out

One of the most effective patterns for improving your week is having consistent times for eating, sleeping, and working out. If you set those in place and work everything else around that, you have a great start and help ensure that you invest in yourself.

This is how many of the most effective people structure their week. They know how much sleep they need; therefore, they make sure they go to bed at the right time for the right amount of hours. They enjoy their meals at allotted times throughout the day: for some it means eating three times a day while others prefer smaller portions five times or more a day. When it comes to exercise, one of the most common patterns for successful people is to work out first thing in the morning. This gives them a continuous block of "me" time from the night before into the start of their day; it also ensures that the workout happens. Another pattern is to work out after work as a way to cap off their work day and transition to home, thus helping to enforce a boundary for ending their work day. Some people work out at the very end of the day if they can't find any other time that works. What's important is making time.

By fixing time for eating, sleeping and working out, you help make sure you take care of the basics. Eventually, you won't have to spend as much time thinking about them as you find ways to improve efficiencies and reduce friction. For example, if you work out in the morning every weekday, you'll find ways to glide into your routine. These three activities are core for your energy and are core energy patterns that support you. When neglected or improperly managed, however, they can work against you.

Carve Out Time for What's Important

You don't have time for things, you make time for things. Your time allocations should match your priorities. If you schedule it, it happens. If you leave it to chance, you'll have random success. The key is to figure out what's important to you and put it on your map. Make it a part of your schedule by design. By making time for things, you'll improve your focus.

Consolidate Related Activities

It's common to have activities spread throughout the week that would be better off done in a batch. Consolidate them. This optimizes your routines and frees up more time. It's task-switching and hopping around that can eat up a lot of your time and lessen your effectiveness.

Consolidate Weaknesses

Activities that make you weak might be scattered throughout your week. Consolidate these as well. For example, consider doing all the activities that make you weak in the first hour of your day when you are your strongest. Likewise, you can push as much of these weakening activities as you can to the start of your week. Compartmentalizing your time like this keeps your energy strong.

Add Strengths

The secret to improving your energy is to add more activities that make you strong throughout your day and week. For example, one technique is to schedule lunches with people you enjoy and that catalyze you. You can also schedule activities you really enjoy to the end of each day and at the end of the week so that you have something to look forward to, and you end on a high note.

Schedule Free Time

If you want to increase your free time, schedule more of it. It might seem strange to schedule your free time, but it will liberate you. For example, if you know a break is scheduled, it's easier to stay fully engaged. Also, it's easier to truly enjoy your free time if you've already allocated time to get the things done that you know you must do.

Drive Your Week

You can either drive your week or you can be randomized and react. **You can drive or be driven.** Driving your week isn't complicated once you know the main techniques. The keys are really to keep balance and to spend more time in your strengths and less time in your weaknesses.

Scan Your Hot Spots

Remember to scan your Hot Spots; they are your balancing point in life. You can create your own Hot Spots, but you can also start with this frame:

- Mind
- Body
- Emotions
- Career
- Financial
- Relationships
- Fun

If you have not done so already, then I recommend reading "Chapter 4 – Hot Spots" to get a good foundation in this basic tenet of Agile Results.

Start with The Rule of 3

When you start your week, simply think of three outcomes or results you want for the week. If you get that done, you can always bite off more, but picking three things will help you prioritize and stay focused, especially once you get in the thick of things. You'll also start to get a better sense of how well you can accomplish what you set out to do.

This might force you to bite off smaller and smaller things until you can get some consistency in your results. The key is to figure out your capacity and to improve your ability to set or reset your own expectations.

Monday Vision, Daily Outcomes, Friday Reflection

The heart of your week is the Monday Vision, Daily Outcomes, Friday Reflection pattern. This is the scaffolding to support your weekly results. It's how you'll get a fresh start each week and each day. It's also how you'll improve over time. It's a simple, yet consistent pattern you can count on. On Mondays, you envision what you'd like to accomplish for the week; you simply imagine—if this was Friday, what three results would you like under your belt? Each day, you figure out three results for the day that help you move towards your three results for the week. At the same time, you stay flexible so that you're always working on the next best thing for you to do. On Fridays, you reflect on your results.

End Your Week

When you end your week, make the most of it. Reflect on your results and carry what you learned forward. Keep the end of your week as simple as possible. Think of it as the downward side of a mountain. Wednesday is hump day for a reason. By the end of the week you should be on your way down from your climb.

Friday Reflection

Carve out a half-hour on Fridays to reflect. Ask yourself what three things are going well and what three things to improve. In addition, take the time to analyze your results against what you set out to do. Are you surprised? What's getting in the way? How might you do it differently? These are opportunities to improve and refine your ability to get results.

Show-and-Tell

End your week with a show-and-tell. This can be for you or for others. It's great to see your results come to fruition. Step through them. If you're on a team, this can be especially valuable as a way to share your results. If you worked hard on something all week, show and share your results. If it is just for you, take the time to really embrace the fact you delivered. Rewarding your own ability to deliver results is how you keep yourself inspired and lessen your dependence on other people to acknowledge you. Your reward will be a job well done.

Improve Your Week

Once you have the basics in place for an effective week, there are a few key practices you can explore for improving your results. The key is to stay balanced and spend more time in strengths and less in weaknesses. It's also about making sure you accomplish what's important to you. Remember that you're not going for productivity (i.e., simply checking things off a list). You are going for meaningful results in your life. It's your life by design.

Increase Your Power Hours

Count your power hours. Your power hours are the times throughout the day when you're most productive: your energy is strong, your mind is clear, and you're in the zone. Plowing through your work is easy and you're in your flow. You find your power hours by paying attention to the points in the day where you get your best results with the least amount of effort. It might even help by first finding your worst parts of the day to identify your non-power hours. If you currently have a handful of power hours over the course of the week, shoot for ten. Increase it from there. You add power hours by changing the activities you do or moving things around in your schedule, until you unblock your best results. Adding power hours is one of the best ways to improve your results for the week.

Increase Your Creative Hours

Just like adding power hours, you might benefit from adding more creative hours. Count how many creative hours you have during the week. If it's not enough, schedule more and set yourself up so that they truly are creative hours. If you're the creative type, this will be especially important. If you don't think of yourself as very creative, then simply think of these as free hours to let your mind wander and explore or reflect.

Schedule Things You Need Time For

Scheduling things is one of the best ways to make sure it happens. This includes giving it the proper amount of time needed. The more realistic you are about how much time things take, the better you get at accomplishing them. The trick, of course, is to find a balance; make time available but also don't spend too much time on things. As one of my mentors put it, "Don't spend 20 dollars on a 5-dollar problem." Make sure the time investment matches the value. Your time is one of the most important resources you have. Invest it wisely.

Add Buffers

Don't let all your activities bump up against each other—have some breathing room. One of the most important buffers is your morning buffer. For example, give yourself more than enough time to get to work. This way you aren't stressed by the traffic and have made allowances for things to go wrong. The more you account for things going wrong, the less stress you'll experience and the less things will actually go wrong. If you run too tight a ship, you'll find things will go wrong more often and throw you off. Life has lots of unexpected curve balls, so allow for them by design.

Avoid All-or-Nothing Thinking

Don't let all-or-nothing thinking ruin things. Don't throw out the baby with the bathwater. Don't let one bad apple spoil the bunch. Things do go wrong, and things will go wrong. Roll with the punches. Having your weekly routines will help you gradually improve and respond to change. It's this learn-and-respond pattern that will see you through each day, each week and each month. It's that pattern that will produce results.

Make Time to Recharge

Renewal is an important part of your cycle. You need to make sure you have the energy to keep going. Therefore, it's important to know what actually recharges you versus what drains you. Some things that drain some people actually recharge other people. Pay attention to how you respond in terms of energy to different activities and find the routines, patterns, and practices that recharge and renew you.

Experiment Between Morning Person and Night Owl

Some people find that they are more creative at night but are more productive during the day. Other people find they simply can't be creative in certain situations or that they can't be productive in others. Experiment between being a night owl and a morning person to see which patterns work best for you. You might even find that these patterns switch, depending on the season. For example, you might prefer to be a night owl in the winter and a morning person in the summer.

In Summary

- Design your week to support you.
- Use the Monday Vision, Daily Outcomes, Friday Reflection pattern to drive your week.
- On Mondays, identity three compelling results for the week.
- On Fridays, reflect on three things going well and three things to improve.
- Baseline your schedule.
- Set boundaries and limits.
- Fix time for eating, sleeping, and working out.
- Consolidate the things that make you weak.
- Add strengths to your week.
- Schedule free time to your week.

Chapter 8 – Design Your Month

Fall seven times, Stand up eight. —Japanese Proverb

In This Chapter

- Learn how to create a scannable map of your month.
- Learn how to design a more effective month.
- Learn how to use The Rule of 3 to keep scope creep at bay.

This chapter shows you how to map out your month for monthly results. Mapping out your month helps you to really prioritize and focus on the most important results. It also helps you see another level up beyond your weekly results. This is especially helpful when you have longer term projects.

Things can take you by surprise. While you can't predict everything, you can improve how you anticipate your month. You do this by mapping it out.

Month at a Glance

Your Month at a Glance should show your queue, each week, and the three top priority outcomes for each week and for the month. The following table is an example template:

Table 8.1 Month at a Glance

Queue	Week	Outcomes	Completed
MUST • •	Week 1	• • •	• • •
• SHOULD •	Week 2	• • •	• • •
• • 	Week 3	• • •	• • •
COULD • • •	Week 4	• • •	• • •

Note how the Queue is organized by MUST, SHOULD, and COULD. This is a helpful way to chunk up your backlog. You can record your results for each week in the Completed column. The template is lightweight by design, allowing you to easily make adjustments without having to spend a lot of time in administration. Don't worry about directly connecting the dots between your daily outcomes, weekly outcomes, and monthly outcomes. Instead, think of each as a different perspective and scope, and they complement each other. They will often align, but the most important thing is that your daily, weekly, and monthly outcomes serve you: helping you stay focused on your next best thing to do and achieve the results you need.

Mapping Out Your Month

The key to mapping out your month is to chunk it down and do a piece at a time. Here is a summary of the flow of steps I take to map out the month:

- Step 1. Make a list of all your outcomes.
- Step 2. Prioritize your list of outcomes.
- Step 3. Assign outcomes to each week.

It really is that simple. Now, let's walk through each step in more detail.

Step 1. Make a List of All Your Outcomes

Make a list of all the outcomes you want for the month. This is where windows of opportunity really matter. Imagine if the month was over, what are all the things you would regret the most if you didn't complete them? Dump everything you can think of. Let the ideas flow freely and don't edit them in this step—just write them down.

Step 2. Prioritize Your List of Outcomes

In this step, you prioritize your list of outcomes. At this point, you probably have a good sized "laundry list." The goal for this step is to chunk up your list of outcomes so your highest priority items float to the top. I recommend chunking it up using the following priorities:

- MUST
- SHOULD
- COULD

I've found that it helps to simply think in terms of MUST, SHOULD, and COULD. MUST is what you must get done, SHOULD would be nice, and COULD is just a pipe dream. Your MUSTs are your next actions; they are immediate and obvious relative to your SHOULDs and COULDs.

I use MUST, SHOULD, and COULD because I find those terms resonate better. Alternatively, you could use priority 1, priority 2, and priority 3 (or p1, p2, and p3). Use what works for you. You know it's working when you're able to identify the most important results based on either impact or windows of opportunity. In fact, missing windows of opportunity is the biggest oversight people make. Time changes what's important. It can also significantly amplify the impact of what you get done, or what you don't get done. There's a lot to be said for "a stitch in time saves nine." When prioritizing, include estimates taking into account the best time to work on specific tasks. Doing so gets you from good results to great.

As you prioritize your list of outcomes, make sure to trim down your MUSTs (or whatever equivalent label you've chosen) to no more than three items. You can always bite off more after you complete your three MUSTs. Priority and focus are your best friends. Your worst enemy is scope creep. Keep it at bay by using The Rule of 3.

Step 3. Assign Outcomes to Each Week

In this step, you assign the three highest priority outcomes for each week. These should work towards your three outcomes for the month. Notice how you can zoom out to the big picture by looking at three results for the month, or you can zoom in to more details by looking at three results for the week. It's this ability to zoom in and out that helps you see the forest from the trees and keeps you focused on your best results.

In Summary

- Think in terms of monthly results.
- Know the 3 most important outcomes for the month.
- Know the 3 most important outcomes for each week.

Chapter 9 – Design Your Year

The best way to predict the future is to create it. —Peter Drucker

In This Chapter
- Figure out your three best results for the year.
- Learn how to create a scannable map of your year at a glance.
- Learn how to design more effective months to support your year.

This chapter helps you achieve three great results for the year. It also helps you see your year at a glance, design a more effective year, and enjoy the journey along the way.

What if you could look back a year from now and say with confidence that you achieved the three most important changes that you could make in your life right now? This could be anything from getting to your ideal weight, to finding your dream job, to taking an incredible journey. That's the idea behind focusing on three great results for the year. It's about having the three most important things to you, for the year, under your belt.

I first learned to focus on three great results for the year by studying goals and objectives. I tried to get precision and accuracy around goals, objectives, strategies, and tactics. When I finally got clarity, I pushed all my thinking aside and asked a very simple question, "If this were next year, what are three great results I would want?" Without hesitation, I answered: (1) get to my fighting weight; (2) finish my book; and (3) take an epic adventure. (Interestingly, completing this chapter means finishing the writing for my book.) Since it sounded almost too simple to be useful, I had to question whether this was how I was going to set my goals for the year. Something inside me told me that I finally found the secret sauce for significant change. I would feel a sense of fulfillment if I turned the page of another year of my life and found that I had achieved these three things for the year (or at least come really close).

Knowing your three great results for the year is one thing. Seeing your year at a glance is another. The inspiration for seeing my year at a glance came from one of my colleagues. He was always calm, cool, and collected. One of his secrets was his calendar on the wall. It was a simple view of the year at a glance. He put all the key project events on it, across multiple projects. He included people on the teams for their input as he mapped out the project milestones, activities, and deliverables. Everybody could easily see the map with the end in mind, and how to get there. They could see and plan for holidays. They could see when there might be bottlenecks or resource constraints. I thought to myself: If this works so great for dealing with complicated projects and dependencies ... why not use it for life? And so, I did.

Three Great Results for the Year

Your three great results for the year are the three most important changes you want in your life at this time. These could be related to your work or personal life. These could be about making your dreams happen, such as starting your own business, or they can be about getting yourself out of pain, such as getting out of debt. Think about your life Hot Spots: mind, body, emotions, career, financial, relationships, and fun. What are the three most important things you want to achieve? The simplest way to get to some insightful answers is to ask yourself the tough question, "If this were next year, what are three things I would want to be different?"

My 3 Great Results

1. Get to my fighting weight.
2. Take an epic adventure.
3. Finish my book.

Figure 9.1
3 Great Results for the Year

For my example, I picked three things:
1. Fighting weight – because I want the feeling of freedom and flexibility.
2. Epic adventure – because I want to test myself and create great experiences to look back on.
3. Book – because it's the greatest gift I can give others—the gift of results.

Grant Yourself 3 Wishes

You can almost think of this as granting yourself three wishes. If you had three wishes to grant yourself, what would you wish for? Dream big before you whittle away to what you think is realistic or possible. You have all year to hone and refine. Listen to your gut instinct. For now, let your inner child say three things you want. You can always change them. You can always refine them. What's important is that you first trust yourself to put out on the table what your three wishes would be. Go ahead and grant yourself these three wishes, but instead of using magic, we're going to use the power of intention and the power of project management to make things happen. By making meaning and assigning significance to each wish or result, you unleash your most resourceful self. **This is the same kid with the big dreams: back before anybody told you what you couldn't do, or worse, before you told yourself what you couldn't do.** By using some simple project management skills, such as planning the results you want and when you want them, you give yourself clarity about the end in mind while staying flexible in how you get there.

Imagine Your Wishes

Briefly imagine what it would be like if you accomplished each of your three wishes or results you want for the year. If the results you imagined don't feel compelling or inspiring, you haven't found your three wishes. Don't work at it. Play at it. What's important is that your three wishes are compelling for you. If you achieve these three things within a year from now, you want to be able to honestly say that you spent your time on the things that matter most to you at this moment in your life.

When you imagine your wishes come true, don't merely see it in your mind's eye—invoke all of your senses. What does it feel like? What does it smell like? What does it sound like? What does it taste like? The "sweet taste of success" isn't just a metaphor. If you have a tough time imagining how it looks, then try this exercise—see it on the big screen. Imagine you're in a theater and you're watching the movie about one of your wishes. The better you can see it, the more you can invoke your other senses, and the more you have working for you.

Here's a quick example. When I decided that the ability to run longer distances was an important result for me, I imagined what it felt like to run free. I imagined a long winding road through the mountains. I imagined the cool, crisp autumn air as I ran through a blaze of trees with sun burnt leaves of orange, red and yellow. I could smell the outdoors so much that I could almost taste the flowers. My body felt so lean and so strong that I didn't have to ask, "Can I make it?" Instead, I simply asked, "Where do I want to go?"

The Why Behind Your Wishes

Once you have chosen your three wishes, the best thing you can do is find out why they matter so much. The simplest way to do this is to just start writing down why they matter. Take each result you want to achieve and write a hearty paragraph about why it really matters to you. Ask yourself, "Why do I need to make this happen?" Don't critique your thoughts. Instead, just pluck your reasons as they flow and plot them down. Think of it as your personal manifesto, and if you should forget why you do what you do or get knocked off your horse, this will be your reminder. If you can't write at least a paragraph of why each one is so important to you and why you need to make it happen, then consider whether you picked your three best results for the year. When you're designing your year, you really want to invest your life force where it matters most.

Test Your 3 Wishes

Know the true result you want to achieve; don't get stuck on how you get there or confuse a means with the ends. By separating the ends from the means, you give yourself flexibility in how you get there. For example, you might think you want a Ferrari. What you might actually want is to feel free or to feel strong. There are plenty of faster, less expensive, and more effective ways than buying the Ferrari. If you think you really need the Ferrari, then try before you buy—rent one for the day. Experiment with your dreams and test them to figure out what you really want. Remember the adage, "Be careful what you wish for, because you just might get it."

Making Your Wishes Happen

When you have your big goals in front of you (and you will because you can easily remember your three wishes), your world suddenly conspires with you. You'll find yourself noticing all sorts of things that you didn't before. Have you ever bought a new car, only to suddenly see the same car on the road when you never noticed how many there were before? Your mind is an amazing filter. By setting your sights and living with focus, you expand your awareness. You start to realize how many people and resources, in addition to your own abilities, are available to help you. In fact, a useful exercise is to simply make a list of all the people, resources, and skills that can help you make your dreams happen.

By clarifying your yearly results, you guide your daily, weekly, and monthly results. By keeping these loosely connected, you allow for change while keeping your eyes on the prize. It's the full power of the Agile Results system working for you. You get a fresh start each day, each week, each month, and each year to make progress against whatever the most important results are in your life. It's this rhythm of results that helps you respond to change while getting results along the way.

Goals Setting and Your 3 Wishes

While focusing on three results or three wishes for the year doesn't necessarily replace your normal goals setting exercise (although it might), you can use it to guide and supplement any other goals setting or planning exercises. It's really about helping you make mindful choices so that another year of your life doesn't slip by where you ask yourself at the end of the year, "How did I let that go?" or, "Why didn't I just focus on that?" Goals and objectives are powerful tools. However, you should be able to see the forest from the trees, and no tool or technique should overshadow your power to dream up great results for your life. That starts inside you, and the key here is just letting it out. You're perfectly free to use all of your tried-and-true goal setting methods. Consider this exercise, however, as the icing on top or as the firm foundation you can use to drive the rest of your goals and objectives from, or anywhere in between. Don't throw out goal setting methods that work for you, but do make sure that you give yourself a chance to dream up and design your best year possible. It's your life—dream big dreams and grant your wishes.

Questions and Answers About Your 3 Results for the Year

While explaining this approach to a friend, he had some questions. I figured the best thing I can do is share those questions with you, along with my answers, since many of you may have the very same questions:

- **Question:** *How do I evaluate goals that are applicable as yearly goals versus monthly?*
- **Answer:** It's OK to be off. You can always adjust, but if you can't do it within the month, it's probably something for the year. Keep in mind that if you finish one of your goals, you can add another. The simplest way to test yourself here is to ask yourself, "If this were next year, what are the top three things I would regret the most if I didn't accomplish them?" Don't live a life of regret. Lead a life of action and results. Like anything, you'll get better with practice. Just thinking in terms of three things that you want to accomplish for the year is a start in the right direction. If you accomplish them in less than a year, then good for you—you're ahead of the game. It's an open buffet, so grab your next three results; just don't bite off more than three at a time. If you start trying to remember your four or five most important things, then you lose the power, perspective, and focus of keeping the three most important results right in front of you.

- **Question:** *How do I track progress against my yearly goals when my monthly goals are derivatives of the yearly, and not the whole goal?*
- **Answer:** The simplest way is to evaluate your monthly results. Simply list your key accomplishments and progress each month. You can then evaluate your immediate results against the bigger picture. Three months in, are you a quarter there? Six months in, are you halfway there? Or, do you have a specific block of time when you'll achieve your results. For example, to take my "epic adventure" I blocked off October as the month to make it happen.

- **Question:** *What are examples of a good yearly goal?*
- **Answer:** When I see people a year later, some of the most profound and meaningful changes are these: a new position or a new job, a new life style, a new house, a new body, a new or improved relationship, a new outlook on life, more smarts or skills at their craft, a new hobby, an epic adventure, etc. Just about any significant change takes more than a day or week or month to accomplish. Other goals could also simply be a change that you want in your life, and you'd like to practice throughout the year. For example, you might want to eat less candy, or you might want to quit smoking. By focusing on a habit, giving yourself a year, and moving toward your outcome each month, you can structure yourself for success. You can also give yourself additional leverage by adding these practices: daily, weekly and monthly results; checking your progress at the end of each month; and using monthly improvement sprints when you need to add focus. Allow for the fact that change is hard. You might fail multiple times; just keep getting back on the horse, learn from each setback, and carry the good forward. Don't break yourself against your own goals by biting off too much or beating yourself over the head with them; instead, use them to lift you and guide your choices.

- **Question:** *How do I properly set boundaries on what a yearly goal encompasses?*
- **Answer:** Worry less about the boundaries and more about being able to say your three great results you want for the year to yourself and to others. You'll naturally find the boundaries during the progression of the year. You'll either be driven by some great pain or by some great pleasure; at which point, you'll need to respond. Like your daily, weekly, and monthly results, your yearly results are flexible and should support you. If work is your biggest pain point, chances are one of your three great results will be about work. If your personal life is a struggle, chances are you'll have at least one of your three great results about your personal life. If you are having trouble finding the right three things, consider a more structured approach: (1) pick one great result for work; (2) pick one great results for home and personal life; and (3) pick one great results from one of your life Hot Spots (mind, body, emotions, career, financial, relationships, and fun).

- **Question:** *Is it appropriate to change a yearly goal mid-year?*
- **Answer:** Yes, and that's actually a key to Agile Results. Agility is about responding to change. The key is making sure you change your goals for the right reasons. Your test is always, "What's the next best thing to accomplish in your life?" To stay out of the short-term trap, check yourself against different time periods. What's the next best thing to accomplish in your life for the next month, the next year or the next ten years? When you check yourself against these different time frames, it quickly changes your perspective on how important something is. For example, eating that cake might feel good right now, but what do you want for yourself for the month or for the year, and does that help you? You can use time frames to bound your goals, prioritize your actions, and correct course. The most important thing is that you are taking action towards your most important results, and you may very well find that you need to change your goals as you get more clarity. You may find that what you thought was a goal was really a means to an end. You might also find that what was important before isn't important now. Time changes what's important. It's also a changing landscape. As things change in your life, you have to respond, driving from the inside out. This is about responding, not reacting, and embracing the fact that life happens, things change, and so can you. If you embrace this, you can make change work for you instead of against you, and look forward to the fresh starts each day, each week, each month, and each year, including fresh goals for your best results.

Year at a Glance

This section shows you how to map out your year to create scannable months. When you can see your months at a glance, you can anticipate better and create better plans—or at least get surprised less. Having a rough idea for your months helps you to feel more empowered and to take steps necessary to improve your monthly results by design.

Mapping Out Your Year

Things can take you by surprise, unless you expect them. While you can't predict everything, you *can* improve how you anticipate your year. You do this by mapping it out.

Recurring Activities

List your recurring monthly activities. For example, you might list seasonal sports you participate in. It's less about being complete, and more about identifying the big things you spend your time on during the year.

Key Events

List any key events. To keep it simple, start with birthdays and holidays. Next, include any of your vacations or big projects. Next, list any events that you participate in. Then, list the big events that impact you. For example, for my work at Microsoft, there are a number of big industry-wide events that I need to be aware of throughout the year. By noting the timing of these events, I can be proactive about preparing content to supply to event coordinators, or at the very least, know when people won't be available to work on my projects. Before I mapped out these events in advance, I was continually surprised, either doing last minute work or losing key people from my projects. Once I started making maps each year, my ability to anticipate improved, making it easier to design my project schedules to accommodate big events.

Meaningful Milestones

A milestone is a significant point in development. They help you chart progress along the way during a larger project. If you already do project work, it will be natural for you to know your big milestones, such as project start, checkpoints along the way, and when you are done. If you don't normally do project work, you can assign milestones to any big task or body of work that you have.

Year at a Glance Templates

The following templates can help you quickly map out your year. You can use a pen and paper, a whiteboard, a spreadsheet, or whatever works best for you. The main idea is to capture a month-by-month picture of your year, including recurring activities, key events, and meaningful milestones.

One template focuses on plotting out the key events for the year. The other templates focuses on plotting out the key outcomes you want for each month. Together, these templates help you organize your thinking and planning for the year. In addition, you can find the Yearly Planner template in the Appendix section of this guide; this template combines capturing your three outcomes for the year, your key outcomes, and your key events all at a glance.

Template – Events for the Year at a Glance

This template is helpful when you need to first map out the big picture of your year. You can quickly plot out birthdays, holidays, vacation, personal projects, and key events. On the work side, include your big projects, recurring events, such as your mid-year and annual reviews, and include any other meaningful milestones that help you see your year at a glance. You may be significantly surprised the first time you do this exercise, unless you had a good picture of your year already.

Table 9.1 Events for the Year Template

Month	Personal	Work
January		
February		
March		
April		
May		
June		
July		
August		
September		

October		
November		
December		

Example

Here is an example of using the Events for the Year template:

Table 9.2 Example of Events for the Year

Month	Personal	Work
January		
February	• Valentine's Day • Baseball season coming. Going to coach?	
March		• Projected release date for Project 1
April		
May		• Budget planning starts for new fiscal year
June	• Spring cleaning once weather is nice • Kids out of school	
July		• Likely that new positions added or cut at work for new year
August		• Annual review
September	• Kids back to school	
October	• Wife's birthday • Sister's birthday • Winterize boats and jet ski	
November	• Thanksgiving with family • Get ready for ski season • Good time to prepare items to sell on eBay for Christmas	

December	• Christmas shopping • Kids school break	• A lot of vacations for people. Expect less support

Template – Outcomes for the Year at a Glance

This template is a list of your activities and outcomes on a month-by-month basis. I find it easier to first identify the results or outcomes that I want for a given month, and then identify the activities that will support that outcome. This tells me where I'll be spending my time. It also puts a stake in the ground. If it looks like I have too many months without flowing the right results, then I can adjust my focus and where I spend my time. Mapping this out also helps me spot bottlenecks and potential problems well before I run into them.

Table 9.3 Outcomes for the Year Template

Month	Outcomes	Activities
January		
February		
March		
April		
May		
June		
July		
August		
September		
October		
November		
December		

Example

Here is an example of using the Outcomes for the Year template:

Table 9.4 Example of Outcomes for the Year

When	Outcomes	Activities
January	• Enjoy skiing	
February	• Be a successful little league coach	• Express interest in coaching
March	• Be a successful little league coach	• Arrange work to make space for baseball practice and games. No travel. • Attend league meetings • Partner with App Arch Team
April	• Be a successful little league coach	• Attend games and practices 3x a week
May	• Be a successful little league coach • Home expanded to add more space for kids	• Set budget for house remodel • Get contractor recommendations and do research to pick one • Research materials with wife • Decide on remodel ordering so kitchen and bathrooms still functioning at all times
June	• Home expanded to add more space for kids	• Finalize remodel plans and permits • Begin construction • Weekly progress review including budget. Make adjustments
July	• House Remodel • Relationship vacation. Three days alone with wife. No kids.	• Complete remodel • Vacation: Decide location. • Vacation: Get tickets or hotel reservations. • Vacation: Make sure kids are taken care of. • Vacation: Plan based on remodel state

August	• House Remodel • Relax with wife	• House Remodel buffer time • Take vacation
September	• Surprise birthday party for wife • Thanksgiving	• Find venue • Talk with friends to invite • Where are we holding Thanksgiving? Decide. If travelling, get tickets.
October	• Surprise birthday party for wife	• Hold party
November	• Good Thanksgiving	• If Thanksgiving at our place, plan so less stress
December	• Life perspective for kids	• Research shelters and food banks. • Schedule time to serve at food bank around holidays

In Summary

- Identify your three key results for the year.
- Create a scannable map of your year at a glance.
- Design more effective months to support your year.

Part III – Results Explained

In This Part:

Chapter 10 – Results Frame, Personas, and Pitfalls

Efficiency is doing things right; effectiveness is doing the right things. —Peter Drucker

In This Chapter
* Learn about the Results Frame and how to use it as a lens for organizing and sharing information in the productivity space.
* Learn key Productivity Personas.
* Learn key Productivity Pitfalls.

The Results Frame provides a backdrop for organizing and sharing principles, patterns, and practices for results; think of it as a map of the territory. The frame itself is simply a set of Hot Spots. You can use the frame to organize your thinking, guide your learning, and provide a place to put new principles, patterns, and practices that you learn for productivity. This helps you evaluate new information while at the same time, reducing information overload. For example, you might find that you have plenty of techniques for task management, but you're missing techniques for focus. By having a frame, you can evaluate your existing body of knowledge for strengths and weaknesses.

The Productivity Personas defines and names a common set of behaviors. By having a name for different personas, you can improve your self-awareness and be deliberate about which persona you choose to use for a given situation. For example, when you need to tackle a tough problem, you might choose your Thinker hat. When you need to take action, you might swap modes from Thinker to Doer. The power of personas is more than just a mental model for behaviors. You can also use the personas to improve teamwork, as well as improve your own effectiveness through more effective pairing. For example, if you're a Starter, find yourself a good Finisher. If you're a Maximizer, find yourself a good Simplifier.

The Productivity Pitfalls are common mistakes that get in the way of results. If you understand and recognize these pitfalls, you can respond more effectively. Awareness is the first step. You may be aware of some of the negative patterns, but this provides a robust set that you can use to identify problems you may be running into. One thing to keep in mind is that some problems may be due to the situation, while other problems may be due to your approach. It's important that you don't internalize situational problems. At the same time, it's also important that you don't think of yourself as a victim. Instead, simply recognize the problem and respond. Responding may simply be changing your expectations, or it may mean changing your approach, or even changing the situation. In any case, you're never helpless. You always control your attitude and response, and that's the most important point.

Results Frame—Hot Spots for Results

If you don't know what you're looking for, you're not going to see it. Chunking up a problem makes it easier to tackle. You can use the following Results Frame to help you make sense of the results space:

Table 10.1 Results Frame

Hot Spot	Description
Action	How you take action and manage your activities towards results.
Efficiency and Effectiveness	How you manage the cost and speed of your results, as well as how you manage the quality of your results.
Energy Management	How you manage your energy in terms of thinking, feeling, and doing, as well as how you take care of your eating, sleeping, and working out.
Expectations	How you set and reset expectations with yourself and others.
Focus	How you focus your time, energy, and attention.
Goals and Objectives	How you set meaningful goals and objectives for your results.
Information Management	How you organize and manage information, as well as avoid information overload.
Learning	How you find the lessons, improve, and correct course.
Mindsets and Motivation	How you get your head in the game.

Planning	How you map out the work to be done.
Prioritizing	How you choose what's more important.
Self-Awareness	How to improve your knowledge about yourself in terms of achieving results.
Self-Discipline	How you correct your behavior.
Task Management	How you manage your tasks and action items.
Time Management	How you manage and schedule your time.

The productivity space is a well-travelled path, but the problem is that some maps are better than others. You can think of the Results Frame as a map of categories or topics that are important—the Hot Spots for results. Each Hot Spot represents an actionable bucket. You can use this frame as a backdrop for finding, organizing and sharing your knowledge about getting results. By using an organizing frame, you can more effectively manage and prioritize large collections of information.

Productivity Personas

Personas are a simple way to share examples of the different types of behaviors. Anybody can be a mix of some or all of the various personas. No persona is good or bad. Some are more effective than others, depending on the situation. The key is to use the personas as a lens on behavior. You can analyze yourself, other people, and common interactions. We all have the capacity for the various behaviors. The trick is to know your preferences and the preferences of others. Here's a set of personas relevant to the results space:

Table 10.2 Productivity Personas

Persona	Notes
Starter	Starts things but doesn't always finish. Their energy comes from thinking up new ideas and kicking things off. Love prototyping an idea, but once they've figured it out, they're ready to move on to something else.
Finisher	Brings things to closure. Effective finishers, complete things and move on. Is a fit and finish type of person. It's finished when they say it's finished.

Thinker	Is an "ideas" person. Thinking is what they do best. Analysis is their game, but doing is somebody else's game. They don't have to act on their thoughts to enjoy them.
Doer	Does their job. They tend to get their job done. They may not come up with new ideas, but they have a preference for taking action.
Simplifier	Finds the simplest path. Strips things down to the minimum. Good enough for now is OK in their book.
Maximizer	Finds the maximum impact.
Critic	Finds the faults. They'll find ways why you can't or why it's wrong. They'll critique themselves, their work, or their ideas. Anything is fair game.
Can Do	Finds a way. Where there's a will, there's a way, and they'll find it. It may not be the optimal solution, but they'll find a workaround.
Opportunist	Finds the opportunity in any situation.
Perfectionist	Treats everything like a work of art. Quality is their name, finishing isn't their game. They'll be done when it's done. It will be done just as soon as it's perfect. Whenever that is.
Details	Loves the details and will want to see things through. Dots the i's and crosses the t's. They're passionate about spreadsheets.
Big Picture	Sees the forest from the trees. Likes the big ideas and doesn't want to get lost in the minutia.
Facts and Figures	Is a numbers person. They want quantifiable measurements. Like Details, they too like spreadsheets.
Controller	Likes to control things. This could be the Doers, the project, or their world.
Tinkerer	Likes to tinker. The world is their sandbox. Dabbles here, dabbles there.
Marketer	Communicates the value. Knows how to sell ideas.
Achiever	Likes to accomplish things.
Randomizer	Turns their latest priority into other people's problems.
Daydreamer	Likes to dream up better ways for better days. They'd rather dream than do. They don't have to act on their dreams to enjoy them.
Procrastinator	Finds way to put off to tomorrow, what they really should do today. They only send belated birthday cards since they know they'll never send them out on time.

3 Ways to Use Productivity Personas

The personas give you a quick way to identify and label patterns of behavior. More importantly, they provide a lens. You can use this lens to help you understand the behavior and preferences of yourself and other people. Here are three ways you can use the Productivity Personas to your advantage:

1. **Know Yourself.** Use the Productivity Personas to know yourself. If you're aware of the personas, you can use them to your advantage. For example, don't let your inner Critic or Perfectionist get in the way of your Doer. Ask yourself, "When am I at my best? Am I more of a Starter or a Finisher? Am I more of a Maximizer or a Simplifier? Am I more of a Thinker or a Doer?"

2. **Team Up.** Use the Productivity Personas to pair up with other people and improve your own effectiveness. You can also use the Productivity Personas to create more effective teams or to optimize teamwork. Ask yourself, "Who can I team up with to get results? How can I build more effective teams? Who should be paired up on the team for best results?"

3. **Improve the Situation.** You can imagine how some behaviors work better with others and how some can create conflict. Swap out for more effective personas based on the scenario. For example, if you really need a Starter for the situation, but you can't break out of Finisher mode, then see if you can find somebody who can play the role. Ask yourself, "What are the best behaviors for the situation?"

Remember to use the Productivity Personas as a lens. The labels are for behaviors, not for limiting or boxing in personalities. Anybody can demonstrate any of the behaviors at any time. The key is to be aware of the preferences, for yourself and others, and to choose more effective behaviors as well as to optimize yourself and others in any situation.

Productivity Pitfalls

There are lots of ways to fall off the path. It's not whether you fall; it's whether you get back up. You can get back up quicker when you recognize the problem. If you suffer from some of these issues and don't know the solution, don't worry. That's what this guide is for. If you get knocked down, you'll get up again, and nobody's going to keep you down—not even you.

Top 5 Productivity Pitfalls

Here are the top five productivity pitfalls that I've seen time and again the limit people's results:

- Pitfall # 1. Analysis paralysis
- Pitfall # 2. Do it when you feel like it
- Pitfall # 3. Don't know the work to be done
- Pitfall # 4. Lack of boundaries
- Pitfall # 5. Perfectionism

Pitfall # 1. Analysis Paralysis

"Analysis paralysis" can be your worst enemy, especially if you're a heavy thinker or you really enjoy analyzing problems. You never think you have enough information to act on the problem and it always seems like there is more you can know. The problem is, that's true and it's a trap. There's a world of difference between dreaming up solutions and actually implementing them. The way out is to start action on the problem, even small steps, so that you gain momentum as well as feedback on your thinking. You might find that all your analysis doesn't actually help when you try to apply it. One way to help balance your analysis with action is to set limits on how much time or energy you'll spend analyzing and giving yourself small time boxes for taking action. I find that either setting a minimum in terms of time that I'll spend taking action or setting a minimum in the quantity of steps that I'll take (e.g., take three actions on the problem today) helps me stay out of analysis paralysis, and make progress on the problem.

Pitfall # 2. Do It When You Feel Like It

"Do it when you feel like it" works against you in a few ways. You don't always feel like doing things, even when they're in your best interest. You can also miss out on a lot of opportunities along the way, while you're waiting for your inspiration. Most importantly, you're missing opportunities to practice and improve your skills. Imagine if competitive athletes only practiced when they felt like it. This pitfall holds back aspiring artists too. While they're waiting for inspiration, they miss opportunities along the way, and then, when inspiration does come along, they don't have the skills to make the most of it. One of the most effective ways to combat the problem is to simply make time for things and schedule your routines. Having a time for things works just like having a place for things. You can use routines to improve your performance and results. Think of it as getting more chances to get better at what you do.

Pitfall # 3. Don't Know the Work to Be Done

"Don't know the work to be done" is another arch-enemy of results. When you don't know the work to be done, you can't estimate the time or energy it will take. When you don't know the work to be done, you don't get the right people doing the right things. When you don't know the work to be done, it's very easy to get yourself in over your head. You can then compound the problem by throwing more time and energy at the problem. When you don't know the work to be done, you can get surprised along the way by things you didn't expect or anticipate, and without a buffer, you may find yourself overwhelmed and downtrodden. One of the best ways to counter this problem is to map out the work. If you don't know the work, ask the people that do or who have done it before. Another countermeasure is to expect the unexpected—keep a buffer of time and energy so that you can respond instead of react.

Pitfall # 4. Lack of Boundaries

"Lack of boundaries" gets in the way of work-life balance. It can be as simple as missing things like breakfast or lunch. It can mean spilling your work over into the weekend. It can mean that your day never ends, and you bleed your work into all area of your life. It can also mean that you push yourself past your own limits. If you find yourself working well past your best energy, working to the point of diminishing returns, then you know exactly what a lack of boundaries feels like. The best countermeasure for a lack of boundaries is to put some simple boundaries in place. For example, start by making time for breakfast, lunch, and dinner. Make time for working out by actually scheduling it. Find your best time for going to sleep and guard it. From there, you can add some boundaries, such as "no work on the weekend" or "no work during the week nights." A friend of mine set a simple rule of "dinner on the table at 5:30 p.m.," and it's helped him stick to his boundaries for years. Setting boundaries doesn't mean there won't be exceptions, but at least you now have a simple framework that supports you. It's scaffolding for sustainable results. The other thing to keep in mind is that things happen in cycles or stages, so you need to stay flexible. For example, during a project ramp up, I expect to spend more time and energy than I usually do at work. This expectation allows me to cross-check that I'm staying balanced and taking care of the basics.

Pitfall # 5. Perfectionism

"Perfectionism" often goes hand in hand with "analysis paralysis." After all, seeking the perfect plan takes a lot of analysis. There are three main problems with "perfectionism." First, the most crippling form of perfectionism is when you don't start something or won't even try because you know you won't be perfect. Second, you never finish something on time because you're busy perfecting it. Third, you beat yourself up over your results instead of appreciate your learning and growth. Beat "perfectionism" by thinking of results as a path, not a destination. Getting something done "good enough" for now, is better than missing the window of opportunity or over-engineering it. Simply by thinking in terms of "versioning" your results can help you balance getting it right with getting it done. Instead of trying to write perfect prose or bullet-proof code the first time through, make the first draft "good enough," then iterate. The key is to iterate on it: create a series of smaller, manageable hurdles, rather than one giant one that you can't jump over.

30 Common Productivity Pitfalls

If you can at least recognize the common Productivity Pitfalls, you will be better prepared to defeat them or avoid them entirely.

Table 10.3 30 Common Productivity Pitfalls

1. Analysis paralysis	11. Do it when you feel like it	21. Lack of demand
2. Big bang	12. Do whatever it takes	22. Learned helplessness
3. Biting off more than you can chew	13. Doing the same thing, expecting different results	23. Limiting beliefs or assumptions
4. Blamer/victim	14. Don't know the work to be done	24. Limiting situation
5. Burnout	15. Externalize instead of internalize	25. Monolith
6. Burning the candle at both ends	16. Friction	26. Watching the scoreboard
7. Churn	17. Getting stuck	27. Not letting go
8. Crossed-expectations	18. It doesn't feel good	28. Perfectionism
9. Death by 1,000 paper cuts	19. Lack of boundaries	29. Throwing time at the problem
10. Do it later	20. Lack of buffer	30. Wrong approach

These pitfalls reflect the most common patterns of problems that I've seen across a wide variety of situations and people when it comes to getting results. The beauty is that many of these Productivity Pitfalls are directly within your control. Simply by knowing what they, recognizing them, and eliminating them from your habits and practices will go a long way toward unleashing your potential.

Summary of the 30 Common Productivity Pitfalls

Here is a brief explanation of some of the most common pitfalls when it comes to productivity and getting results:

1. **Analysis paralysis.** You think you can ... you think you can ... or can you?... or what about this way ... or that way?... or what about ...? Well, back to the drawing board ...
2. **Big bang.** Rather than delivering value along the way, you wait until the very end—only to find out that you've missed the mark, you lost interest along the way, or worse, your supporters lost interest and trust.

3. **Biting off more than you can chew.** Maybe you think you really can boil the ocean. Maybe it's just your aim to please people where you just can't say no. You'll eventually let them down, just not up front.

4. **Blamer/victim.** It's their fault. Why does it always happen to you?

5. **Burnout.** Burnout is when you shut down. It happens when you keep trying to solve the same problem, but you don't feel like you're making progress.

6. **Burning the candle at both ends.** You rob Peter to pay Paul. Downtime is for wimps. All you need is some more caffeine. Any free time is more time to burn the candle.

7. **Churn.** Churn is when you spin your wheels against a problem but don't make progress.

8. **Crossed-expectations.** This is when you let yourself down, or you let somebody else down. You either failed to reset expectations, or the expectations weren't accurate.

9. **Death by a thousand paper cuts.** Click ... scroll ... click ... scroll ... click ... scroll ... click ... scroll ... ah, there's that file that you use every day! It's not a lot of overhead. It's just a little—about a thousand times a day.

10. **Do it later.** Later never comes, or when it does, something else is more important. A little now might be better than nothing later.

11. **Do it when you feel like it.** You'll do it when you feel the inspiration. You don't need to make time for it; you'll just wait and then strike when the iron is hot.

12. **Do whatever it takes.** You'll step on whomever or whatever you have to. You'll spend every last bit of your precious life force trying to pull it off.

13. **Doing the same thing, expecting different results.** You hit a ceiling, but you keep doing the same thing.

14. **Don't know the work to be done.** You don't know the work to be done. This means you don't know how much effort or time it might take. This also means you don't even know who whom to ask for help. When things go wrong and if you don't know any better, you might end up thinking the world is out to get you.

15. **Externalize instead of internalize.** No satisfaction, just applause or money. Sure you used to enjoy it, but now it's all about the rewards. Doing a good job used to be its own reward. It's more

important what other people say than how you feel about the work you do.

16. **Friction.** It's just a little too much resistance. You barely notice it, but it adds up. Instead of creating a glide path, you ignore the friction. Gradually, the friction snowballs.

17. **Getting stuck.** Congratulations—you found your ceiling!

18. **It doesn't feel good.** You haven't really thought about it, but you just gradually stop doing it. You know you really should do it, but it just doesn't feel good. You thought you could talk yourself into it, and that worked for a while, but now you'd rather do nothing than something that just doesn't feel good.

19. **Lack of boundaries.** Work spills into the weekends. The workday spills into the night. Time for your body or for your mind gets monopolized by time on your work. When you're playing you're thinking about working and when you're working you're thinking about playing.

20. **Lack of buffer.** One more straw will break your back. Go ahead just let somebody try and ask you to do just one more thing. You'll be fine ... as long as everything goes just right, and nothing changes for the foreseeable future ...

21. **Lack of demand.** You let your supply side get in the way of the demand side. There's no demand, but you think there should be. You get mad when nobody appreciates all the hard work you did, that nobody asked you to do to begin with.

22. **Learned helplessness.** What's the use in trying? All you get is pain. This is the worst place to be. This is when you tell yourself that no matter what you do, it won't work. You basically shut down and stop trying. There are lots of ways to end up here, but more importantly you need to know how to get out. The keys to getting out are taking action, changing your approach, and learning from what works.

23. **Limiting beliefs or assumptions.** You limit yourself. Worse, you limit other people. You're pretty sure you can't do it though you never tried.

24. **Limiting situation.** Your container limits your results. Sometimes work is a limiting container. Sometimes how you think about or frame the situation becomes a self-imposed limitation. Limiting metaphors are a good example. It's easy to put yourself in a box.

25. **Monolith.** Bigger is better!... and more complex ... and a little tougher to finish ... and tougher to fix ... and no way are you doing it over—it's too big and too complex!

26. **Watching the scoreboard.** You keep your eye on the scoreboard. The problem is, that's not where you focus should be. The saying is, "Keep your eye on the ball."

27. **Not letting go.** It's not working, but you hold on. It's not serving you, but it's a habit you carry forward. The more you hold on, the tougher it is to let go, the worse the situation stays broken.

28. **Perfectionism.** It's never good enough. If you can't be the best, you never start ... or you never finish on time ... or you never finish at all. And more likely than not, you're too busy beating yourself up to carry what you did accomplish forward.

29. **Throwing time at the problem.** It will be done when it's done. You perpetually miss deadlines, or worse, you continually meet deadlines, at the expense of other areas of your life.

30. **Wrong approach.** You've got the right idea, just not the right approach. Lots of energy, lots of time, no results. You throw more motivation at it, but your hammer just won't turn the screw.

Knowing Is More Than Half the Battle

Chances are that as you read the Productivity Personas and the Productivity Pitfalls, you identify with some of them. Once you recognize something, it's easier to change it if it's not working for you. You can change different things about you. For example, you can change your thinking, feeling or doing. For the situation, you can choose to adapt yourself to the situation, adjust the situation to better suit you, or you can try and avoid those situations all together.

Principles, Patterns, and Practices for Results

One of the most effective ways I've found for finding, sharing, and mapping out large bodies of knowledge is to use principles, patterns, and practices. You can think of a principle simply as a guideline or as a fundamental law or how something works. For example, a principle might be "fix time, flex scope" which means set up time for things and bite off less to fit within the chunk of time that you have. As an underlying principle, this simple guideline might serve as the foundation for many other guidelines. You can think of patterns in a couple ways. A pattern might simply be a tendency or set of acts that you observe (i.e., a behavior pattern). You can also think of a pattern as a problem and solution pair, where the pattern itself is the name of the solution. For example, "flow" is a pattern where you are fully engaged in an activity. The power of patterns is that by naming them, you can share solutions more effectively. You can think of practices as simply methods or techniques. It's a "how" or a "way" to do something. For example, scheduling results is an effective practice. It's a way to make sure you have time for things you need to do, versus just hoping they get done.

Collectively, by thinking about results in terms of principles, patterns, and practices, you can create and grow your personal knowledge base for getting results.

Putting It All Together

When it comes to getting results, you want to consider both your system and your knowledge. The system side is your approach or process (such as Agile Results); it's your habits and practices that you use to get the results you're getting in your life. Ideally, you enjoy the process of getting the results you want, in addition to the results themselves. On the knowledge side, the Results Frame is a simple way to map out and organize how you think about getting results. It's also a way to organize your principles, patterns, and practices for getting results. The Productivity Personas help you understand behaviors, which can limit or amplify your impact and results. The Productivity Pitfalls give you a lens for looking at common sticking points or bottlenecks to your best results.

By improving your knowledge of principles, patterns, and practices for getting results and by continuously improving your system for getting results, you unleash your best results.

In Summary

- The Results Frame is a set of Hot Spots to help you analyze and learn information in the productivity space.
- Use the Results Frame to find actionable principles, patterns, and practices for improving results.

Chapter 11 – 25 Keys to Results

Words may show a man's wit but actions his meaning.
—Benjamin Franklin

In This Chapter

- Learn the sweet spot for results.
- Learn a conceptual model for competency.
- Learn the difference between "above the line" and "below the line."

This chapter helps you get some quick fundamentals of results under your belt.

Results and productivity go hand in hand, but there's a difference. Understanding this difference helps you shift from thinking about efficiency to focusing more on effectiveness. By focusing on effectiveness, you end up improving your efficiency. You also end up paying attention to the results you're getting. It's less about figuring out the right things to do up front and more about taking action and making course corrections based on feedback. This is the secret behind the most successful people. They may make a lot of mistakes. But they turn their failures into lessons. They learn how to make the most of what they've got and they keep taking action, tuning and pruning their abilities as they go. They drop the stuff that's not working and stick with the right things, even when it's tough to do so. They stay committed to their outcomes, but flexible in their approach. This is the ultimate key to success.

This chapter is an overview of some of the key concepts for getting results. If you know some of the underlying concepts, you'll be able to handle resistance more effectively. For example, you might realize that you're simply in an early stage of competency. By knowing the concepts, you can also figure out more effective strategies. Or perhaps you're investing a lot of time and energy, but not producing the results you expect; examine whether you're working on stuff that's not valued. You also might realize that maybe you don't have effective boundaries.

The 25 Keys to Results

Here's a set of 25 powerful lessons on being effective and getting results. Some will be more obvious than others. Some will be counter-intuitive. You don't have to memorize the concepts. Simply familiarize yourself with the ideas. Doing so will provide a firm foundation for your personal productivity practices and results routines.

Key 1: Results over Productivity

In my experience, I've found that *productivity* tends to be associated with "doing more." In contrast, *results* tend to be associated with more meaning and significance: "What did you accomplish? What matters? Is it working?" Therefore, focus more on results; don't just do more things for the sake of doing. Instead of using efficiency as the ultimate measure of success, make it more about effectiveness, value, and impact—now that's getting results!

Key 2: Approach over Results

Just like you can't control all the events in your life, you can't control your outcomes. What you can control is your attitude, your approach, and your response. You can make your best play in each scenario. This is an important distinction. If you focus on the scoreboard, you're not focusing on your actions. Keep your eye on your actions and let the score take care of itself. You'll win some. You'll lose some. And you'll learn a lot. Most importantly, you'll have an internal gauge of your performance.

Key 3: Value Is in the Eye of the Beholder

One common pitfall is throwing a lot of time and effort at things, only to find that when you're done, nobody cares. If you keep feeling a lack of appreciation, then ask yourself, "Who was I doing it for?" If it was for yourself, was it what you most cared about, or could you have invested the same time in something else and felt like you made a more important impact. If you were doing it for somebody else, ask them whether what you're working on is really the most important thing to them. If you're working on a lot of low-priority items, don't expect to get the rewards. In fact, a pattern is that the more you work on low-priority items, the more you become a dumping ground. The more you become a dumping ground, the busier you get; the busier you get, the more overloaded you will feel. Now the worst happens—you're overworked, underappreciated, and no fun to be around. By failing to work on what's valuable and by failing to understand and reset expectations, you've worked yourself into an unrewarding, high-stress scenario.

Key 4: The Sweet Spot—Talent, Passion, and Value

One of the secrets of happiness is doing what you love, or loving what you do. Passion is the ultimate driver. Chances are if you look to your best strengths, you'll find some of your passions. The sweet spot for results is the intersection of talent, passion, and value.

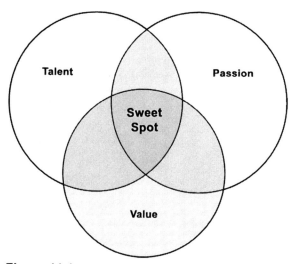

Figure 11.1
The Sweet Spot for Results

Key 5: Efficiency and Effectiveness

Efficiency is doing things better. Effectiveness is doing the right things. The key is to be both effective and efficient. You get there by working first on effectiveness. If something's not working, change your approach. Once you're doing the right things, work on improving your efficiency. You can improve your efficiency through repetition and modeling from successful people. It's also important to have a tight feedback loop.

Key 6: Meaningful Work

Meaningful outcomes are the foundation of meaningful work. Meaningful outcomes help guide your work. If you have a vision for the end in mind, then you have something to work towards. To figure out meaningful outcomes, you ask yourself what you want to accomplish. One of the challenges is when it feels like your work has no meaning. You're the ultimate filter for everything that happens in your life. You assign the meaning to your work. Make the work meaningful. One way to create meaning is to master your craft. Do so by focusing on continuous learning and improvement. Teaching your craft and being a mentor for others is another way to both amplify your learning and your impact.

Work on stuff that's valued. This makes work more meaningful. You should be aware whether it's valued by you, your employer, or your customer. It's fine if it's valuable to you but nobody else, but be aware of it. You may be in the wrong line of work or working on the wrong thing.

Key 7: Mindset and Motivation

Mindset plus behaviors shape your actions and your results. Your mindset has a lot to do with how you'll pace yourself, how you'll gauge your progress, how you'll work through resistance, how much you'll enjoy the work, and how much energy you'll bring to the table. Is this a sprint or a marathon? Are you chipping away at the stone or blasting dynamite? Do you focus on one pitch at a time or getting as much done as possible? Your mindset will be shaped by the metaphors you use to guide you.

Motivation includes the drivers and the why behind your actions. Your motivation will give you the extra energy to produce amazing results. It's the why behind your actions that will either lift you or suppress you. The key to effective results is having a compelling "Why." A compelling "Why" will also help pick you back up when you get knocked down.

Key 8: Motivation and Technique

One of my mentors once told me that motivation is not enough. You need technique. If you have motivation without technique, you're just a motivated idiot. If you have great technique, but no motivation, you won't accomplish anything. But if you have motivation *and* technique, you can produce great results.

Key 9: Boundaries Are Your Friend

Boundaries are the limits you set. Some of the most effective boundaries you can set are time boundaries. For instance, you can set a minimum of time you'll spend improving your body each week. You can set a maximum of time you'll spend working each week. You can set a minimum of time you'll spend on working your relationships each week.

Key 10: Time, Energy, and Technique

Where you spend your time is one part of results. The techniques that you use and the energy you bring are the other parts. Your best results will be the intersection of your time, energy, and techniques. The important point here is that just throwing time at a problem isn't the most effective solution. Just throwing energy at a problem isn't the best solution either. The right techniques can dramatically reduce your time and effort, while amplifying your results.

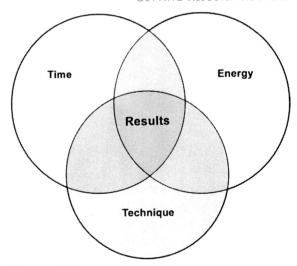

Figure 11.2
Time, Energy, and Technique

Key 11: Above the Line or Below the Line

Some things you do will be "value-add." Others will just be expected. You need to consider whether the work you do is "above the line" or "below the line." Work that's "above the line" is considered value-add. Value is in the eye of the beholder. Work that's "below the line" is just expected. It's like treading water. The funny thing about "below the line" work is that doing more of it won't get you ahead, but not doing it will likely cause you pain. Some people call this "the cost of doing business" or "the tax you pay."

Valued and Expected

Here's a figure to help you visualize the concept of "above the line" and "below the line."

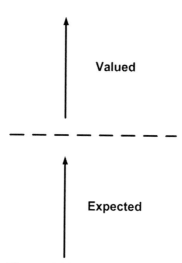

Figure 11.3
Valued and Expected

In the figure, the dotted line separates what's expected from what's valued. If you want to maximize your impact, you need to first take care of what's expected, and then focus on value "above the line."

Above the Line—Valued

Here's a figure to help you visualize "above the line."

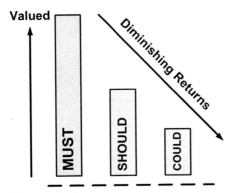

Figure 11.4
Above the Line

Note that even in "above the line" work, you should still prioritize to maximize value to yourself or others.

Below the Line—Expected

Here's a figure to help you visualize "below the line."

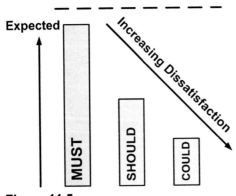

Figure 11.5
Below the Line

Note that in "below the line" work, it's especially important to prioritize. If you miss the important things, they can dramatically take away from your perceived value or your ability to thrive.

Some points to ponder:

- *Is the work that you do considered "above the line" or "below the line"?*
- *Where are you at in terms of achieving results: "above the line" or "below the line"?*
- *Are you working on stuff that's valued?*
- *Who is the value for: you or somebody else?*

The important thing is for you to have an appropriate frame of reference for the value of what you're doing. If you don't feel appreciated for what you're doing, this might be "below the line" to somebody else. You also might find that you're stuck taking care of everything that's "below the line" and you can't get your head above water. The fix is usually reprioritizing what's on your plate, figuring out what the real values and expectations are, and resetting expectations with yourself and others. The last place you want to be is grinding away on something that neither you nor anyone else will value, or worse, missing basic expectations that minimizes your overall effectiveness.

Key 12: Manage Your Plate

Don't overflow your plate. It slows you down, mentally, physically, and emotionally. Instead, clear your plate faster and go up for seconds. You'll build momentum. To manage your plate effectively, this means you have to learn your own capacity. Develop a habit of defining buffers for the unexpected. Each day can bring new opportunities or new priorities. Buffers allow you to welcome and act on the opportunities if you choose to.

Key 13: From Unconscious Incompetence to Unconscious Competence

There is a popular concept in psychology that explains stages of competence. Here are the four stages:

1. **Unconscious Incompetence.** You don't know what you don't know.
2. **Conscious Incompetence.** Now you know what you don't know.
3. **Conscious Competence.** You can think your way through an exercise and perform it with some conscious effort.
4. **Unconscious Competence.** You can perform the task without thinking about it. It's automatic. It's burned into your body and it just knows what to do.

Have you ever noticed how some things you just don't have to think about? For instance, if you drive a stick shift, you don't have to think about shifting gears. You don't have to think your way through it—that's unconscious competence. However, when you first learned, it required a lot of effort because you had to think through every move. Think in terms of these four stages—unconscious incompetence, conscious incompetence, conscious competence, and unconscious competence—when you're learning a new skill.

Key 14: 3 Levels of Learning

You can think of learning something in terms of three levels of learning:

- **Level 1: Intellectual.** You understand it intellectually.
- **Level 2: Emotional.** You have an emotional connection to it.
- **Level 3: Physical.** It's burned into your body.

When you first learn something, you do so at the intellectual level. You can regurgitate the information. You can think through it logically. As you build experiences, you'll form emotional connections to the information. You'll feel a certain way about it. With enough practice and repetition, you'll burn things in at the physical level. Your body just knows what to do.

Key 15: Spend 80% on Action, 20% on Thinking

The idea is to shift from more thinking to more doing. Rather than spending 80 percent of your time thinking and 20 percent doing, spend 80 percent doing and 20 percent thinking. Have a bias for action. You'll act on more of your ideas. You'll get more feedback from yourself and others. You'll improve your habits. A ship at anchor can't course-correct, but a ship in motion can.

Key 16: Factor Thinking from Doing

Think ... think ... think ... think ... think ... This is analysis paralysis. You're stuck in thought mode. Or worse, you're second-guessing yourself every step of the way. You slow yourself down when you think through everything you do. Combat analysis paralysis by thinking *and then acting*. Decide and go. You can analyze your results and change your approach, but don't slow yourself down in the process. If you have a habit of spending all your time thinking, but no time on doing, then try giving yourself time limits. You can also use quantity limits. For example, you might start with three actions you can do with this idea.

Key 17: Results Build Momentum

First, let's look at what happens when you don't get results. When you don't get results, you start to doubt yourself. Worse, you start to feel drained because it feels like your efforts aren't working. Next, other people start to doubt you, and it's a downward spiral. Now, let's look at what happens when you produce results. It feels good. Results, even just small wins, build your confidence. Momentum builds. Like a snowball that grows larger as it rolls, one success builds on another. Another effect is that getting results in one area tends to lead to results in another.

Key 18: It's What You Know and Who You Know

One of the most effective ways to improve your results through who you know is know the gate keepers or the influencers or opinion leaders. The gate keepers are people who control resources, opportunities, money, etc. The influencers and opinion leaders are the ones who people ultimately look to for decisions.

Being good enough isn't good enough. The people in your life can create or limit opportunities. If you keep bumping into ceilings, you might be trying to go it alone. Life's a team sport, and it's better together. You're the sum of your network, and in today's landscape, your network will open or close doors for you. Life's not static and neither is your network. Tune it and prune it like a Bonsai tree. Add the catalysts to your life, and limit the time you spend with the drains.

People are your greatest resource. You won't have time to master everything. Instead, leverage people. People can be for you or against you. If they're for you, they make things easier. If they're against you, they'll drag their feet or make you have to work too hard or block you.

Key 19: Actions Speak Louder Than Words

All talk, no action, takes away your power. You can think of power as your ability to act. However, while actions may speak louder than words, that doesn't mean they will always be heard. Sometimes you need to shout about your work (without being arrogant). You can do so by sharing the knowledge to the benefit of others, sharing it for free without asking for reward, or by at least raising awareness of it in some form or another. Too many people hope their work will be seen, but it needs to stand out from the crowd to be recognized.

Key 20: You Can't Argue with Results

When you wonder whether something is possible or what might work, it's tough to argue with results. If you can find a working example or point to tangible results, you save yourself a lot of time and wasted energy. Results make a good argument. While results don't justify the means, they show a possible outcome. You can evaluate that outcome against what you want to accomplish. If it's a match, then you can work backwards from what works, and find some potential paths.

Key 21: Change Happens

The only constant is change. Life's not static. You're not static. Your situation is not static. There are two things you can do here:

1. Change your mindset to embrace change.
2. Build your anticipation skills.

By anticipating change, and expecting it, you can treat change as an opportunity. If you find yourself constantly reacting to change, that means you're not in a good enough vantage point to see what's going on in the systems you're in. One of the ways to break out of a perpetual reaction loop is to start to identify recurring events that happen throughout the year. Write them down so you can see the year at a glance. You'll notice that the most significant changes are during key events. What might appear to be out of thin air, was actually a progression in a system that you just weren't aware of. You won't anticipate everything, but it's this gradual improvement of anticipation, your mindset of embracing change, and your ability to respond to the unexpected that will dramatically change your feeling of empowerment as well as your personal effectiveness in more scenarios.

Key 22: Passion Is Your Fuel

Energy flows where your passion goes. If you're continuously run down, it's likely that you're spending too much time on things you don't enjoy. Either follow your passion, or find a way to enjoy what you do. One way to enjoy what you already do is to come up with a new mental model or metaphor. For instance, you might think of it as mastering your craft. Another way is to spend more time in other areas that you do enjoy, to help you refuel.

Key 23: You Get What You Focus On

When you know what you're looking for, you start to see more of it. Your brain can only focus on so much at a time. Once you tell your brain something is important, it gets resourceful. You'll suddenly notice more opportunities showing up all around you. Think of it as a lens. The opportunities were there, but now they're in focus. Part of the reason why this works is because of your Reticular Activating

System (RAS): a filter system for your consciousness that brings relevant information to your attention.

Key 24: Leadership Is Influence

John Maxwell teaches us that leadership is influence. If you improve your influence, you amplify your impact. Influence includes your ability to get other people to follow. While you can always make things happen without other people on board, this creates resistance. Resistance wears you down. On the other hand, when you know how to influence effectively, and this includes one on one as well as influencing a room or a team or a crowd, you set yourself up for success. People help you instead of block you or make things difficult.

Key 25: Metaphors Shape Your Experience

You're the most important meaning maker. How you make meaning largely has to do with your self-talk, including the words you use and the pictures you paint. You can think of metaphors as emotional picture words. They can lift you up or bring you down.

In Summary

- The 25 keys represent cornerstone concepts for getting results.
- Know that value is in the eye of the beholder.
- Find the sweet spot for results by blending talent, passion, and value.
- For more effective results, blend time, energy, and technique.
- Efficiency is doing things better, while effectiveness is doing the right things.
- Pay attention to the results you're getting. If it's not working, change your approach.
- Combine motivation and technique to produce more effective results.
- Manage your plate by biting off what you can chew, and having a buffer.
- Invest more time taking action.
- Embrace change and build your anticipation skills.
- Create effective metaphors to motivate yourself or others.

Chapter 12 – 25 Strategies for Results

If you do not change direction, you may end up where you are heading. —Lao Tzu

In This Chapter

- Learn how to treat time as a valuable and limited resource.
- Learn how to improve your results by changing your mindsets.
- Learn how to create a more enjoyable path on your way to your results.

This chapter helps you fill your playbook with some time-tested strategies for getting results. These strategies complement the 25 Keys to Results found in Chapter 11.

Strategies are a big picture perspective while tactics are a small picture perspective. You can think of the strategies as guiding approaches: they guide your tactics while you pursue your goals. You can use strategies to help design your approaches and to evaluate potential practices, methods or techniques. Mix and match strategies, but keep in mind that sometimes strategies support each other, while other times they are competing. Ultimately, you must map relevant strategies to your situation. Rather than try to decide or buy into a strategy, find a way to test and judge it based on your results.

What you don't know can hurt you and knowing the right strategies is like knowing the playbook. While each strategy is independent, many of them work better together. Instead of trying to memorize or implement all of these strategies, simply familiarize yourself with the set and draw from them as needed. One way to get started is to identify three strategies that are most helpful for you now. As you read the strategies, pay particular attention to the ones that you aren't familiar with, since they might be new ways for you to tackle old challenges. Changing your strategies can be one of the best ways to get unblocked or to unleash your potential.

The 25 Strategies for Results

The strategies are a culmination and integration of many lessons learned over many people. These lessons show up time and again in various contexts. The common theme across them is that they can make a significant difference in your ability to accomplish the results you want. What you do with them is up to you. Knowing is often half the battle and there's a good chance that some of the strategies may surprise you.

Strategy 1: Outcomes over Activities

An outcome is result or consequence. An activity is a pursuit in which you're active. Work backwards from the end in mind by figuring out the outcomes you want to accomplish. If you focus on activities, might do a lot, but accomplish little. For example, let's say you're reflecting on your results for this last month. If you start listing all your activities, so what? That's a bunch of activity. What did you actually accomplish or achieve or make progress on or improve? Those are your outcomes.

One simple way to train your mind to switch to focus on outcomes is asking yourself, "What do you want to accomplish?" The trap you can fall into is asking yourself, "What are you trying to do?" I originally learned this distinction when I worked in Microsoft Developer Support. Time and again, I made the mistake of asking a customer, "What are you trying to do?" So, we'd fix the wrong problems. Often they were doing one thing, but trying to accomplish another. Asking "What are you trying to accomplish?" might sound subtle, but it's a big difference in results. The key take away is that if you know where you want to go, there's lots of ways to get there. Be committed to your outcome, but stay flexible in your approach. This lesson shows up time and again.

Strategy 2: Goals Are Vehicles

Always remember that goals are vehicles. They are a means to an end. While reaching for a goal, you become something more. That's why you want goals that stretch you.

SMART Goals

SMART is an acronym to help you improve your goals:

- S = Specific
- M = Measurable
- A = Actionable
- R = Realistic
- T = Timely

You support yourself better by creating specific, measurable, actionable, realistic, timely goals.

Strategy 3: Know the System

When you need to produce results, one of the best things to do is figure out the system. This includes the people involved, the activities involved, and the key triggers or events. If you know how things work, you know where you fit in. You also know who needs to be involved when you need to get things done. If you don't know the system, you can end up fighting unnecessary battles or doing things at the wrong time or just plain working too hard to produce results. Instead, find a way to make the system work for you.

Leverage the System

One of the most important strategies is to leverage the system rather than work against it. When you figure out the system, part of your job is to figure out the key levers you can pull. Sometimes, it's as simple as knowing when to try and pull things off.

Strategy 4: Know the Cycle

Sometimes time is not on your side. Other times, it is. There are a lot of relevant analogies and metaphors here: ebb and flow, wax and wane, off season and on season, high tide and low tide, bull and bear. Cycles and rhythms can dramatically impact the success of what you do. Have you ever tried to swim against the tide? If you know the rhythms and know the cycles you can make them work to your advantage or at least set better expectations. A lot of failures aren't the result of bad ideas, but a consequence of bad timing. You might have experienced the downside of this when you either had an idea the market wasn't ready for or you did too little too late. You might have experienced the upside of this when everything just seemed to go your way and you were riding a wave.

Know Your Own Rhythms

Most people have an off season and an on season. For example, I tend to be more on in the spring and fall and more off in the summer and winter. I know that I also go through bursts of learning and growth, while other times, I'm more on a plateau and have to work hard at it. By recognizing the cycle I'm in, I can better time my plans. I could fight myself or I can work with my natural tendencies. In this case, it's far more effective to work with my tendencies. I don't mind working extra hours in the winter. I do mind working extra hours in the summer. As such, I move some heavy rocks in the winter to set myself up for great results throughout the spring. I don't plan on being brilliant in the summer, but if it happens, great. While I could change my patterns, I've found it's better to first figure out what they are and leverage them, then, if it's not working, figure out what to change. Use well-timed strategies to leverage yourself.

Strategy 5: Treat Time as a Valuable Resource

You can't buy more time. You can, however, spend it more wisely. Time is the main ingredient in life. If you value your time, others will too. If you waste your time, others will too. One of the most important factors in your consistent success is how you treat time. In order to thrive, you must spend time in things that make you strong, make you happy, and keep you growing. Think of yourself as the main manager of your time. Ultimately, you get what you spend your time in. A friend who does marathons says, she gets results by putting in her hours.

Make Time for Priorities

Stephen Covey teaches us to make time for the big rocks. What are your big rocks? In the big picture, start with your basics: mind, body, emotions, career, financial, relationships, and fun. They support each other. For example, it's tough to be great on the job if you don't get enough sleep. It's tough to give your best if you never have fun. If you don't invest in your relationships you can miss out on fun and you can make life difficult for yourself on the job. You must make time for each of these. Make thoughtful decisions in how you invest your time. For example, invest a minimum of two hours a week on your body. Consider investing a minimum of five hours on your relationships. Your circumstances will influence what makes the most sense, but the key is to not over-invest in one area at the expense of another. You can also use time limits as a shutoff valve, such as when you're spending too much time on the job.

Make Time for Yourself

People that make time for themselves tend to operate better. They get clarity in their thinking. They have a better idea of what they want and what they don't want. They figure out ways to fix things that aren't working and they come up with new things to try. They feel more in control of their life and don't feel like they are in constant reaction to the world around them. They are more deliberate about gradually making their world, the way they want it to be.

Make Free Time

Whether you think of it as down time, free time, or whatever, this is your discretionary budget of time to spend on whatever you want. Scheduling your free time might sound like over-engineering, yet it's an exercise that can improve your life. Failing to define free time in your schedule may result in having no buffers, and then it's too easy to get over-extended.

Strategy 6: Fix Time, Flex Scope

Several years ago my circumstances demanded a new way to think about time and scope. I had multiple vendors on my projects and their time was fixed at 40 hours. That meant that when the rest of the team went above and beyond it didn't help because the core team was out of synch. To optimize the results, I had to optimize the team around a 40-hour work week. Interestingly, this turns out to be an Extreme Programming practice. Effective 40-hour work weeks beat inefficient 50, 60, 70, 80-hour work weeks. Fixing time leads to improved time management, better energy management, improved techniques, and ultimately better results. We fixed time, but flexed scope. We bit off what we could chew and prioritized value. It's that simple.

Prioritizing Gets Easier

Here's the deal. If you fix time, but flex scope, you'll improve your success in many areas of your life. For example, you might set a boundary of a 40-hour work week. Now, instead of throwing more time at the problem, you're forced to produce results in a fixed set of time. Your world changes. You prioritize your meetings. You're more deliberate about how you spend your discretionary time. You start to set limits within your day. For example, instead of spending three hours on email, you decide to spend one or less.

Better Techniques

Now, the most important thing happens. You start to question the efficiency and effectiveness of your techniques. Before you threw time at the problem and you never really noticed how ineffective and inefficient your approach was. Now, with time as a constant, you can test different approaches to see what works best.

Energy Up

When you fix time, your energy goes up. There's always an end in sight. You can sprint when you can see the finish line.

The End of Scope Creep

If you flex time, then the tendency is to overflow your plate. Why say no if you'll get to it in the future? You're not sure when and you're not sure how, but you'll get to it. That's how it starts. Next, things fall off your plate, or worse, you throw more time at them to get them done. You routinely cut into your nights and weekends and wonder about that myth called work life balance. Now, consider the opposite. If time is fixed, you have a rough idea of how much to bite off. When you're not sure, you chunk it down. Finish what's on your plate before going up for more. This builds momentum.

When you fix time, you hit more windows of opportunity. You become more reliable to yourself and other people, because you stop biting off what you can't chew. You get in touch with your capacity.

Strategy 7: Diversify Your Results

This works hand-in-hand with fixing time and flexing scope. You can think of your results as a portfolio. It matters where you spend your time and energy. You spread your life force across certain investments. Set minimums and maximums. Take a lot at where you're over-investing and under investing. For example, you might establish a maximum number of hours in your career, and a minimum number of hours on your health each week. If your relationships are slipping, seize the opportunity to carve out more time for them. You'll find that you get more of what you focus on and more of what you spend time and energy on.

Life Frame, Work Projects, Personal Projects

You can diversify your results at multiple levels. For example, consider the following opportunities:

- **Life Frame:** *How can you carve up your overall time across your mind, body, emotions, career, financial, relationships, and fun?*
- **Work Projects:** *How can you carve up your time for administration, think time, and execution time on a daily basis?*
- **Personal Projects:** *How can you carve up your time for your personal projects and make progress on the ones that are most important to you?*

When you diversify your results, you spread your risk. It's all about trade-offs. Don't trade your health for your wealth, or you'll later trade your wealth for your health. Prioritize the vital few things that matter most, and don't neglect areas that really need your attention. Simply having a mental model to look at your portfolio of results is the first step to dramatically improving your effectiveness. It forces you to be more deliberate in how you spread your life force across your portfolio.

It's a Numbers Game

Another important reason to diversify your results is because it's a numbers game. It's hard to predict when things won't work out. Sometimes, the time just wasn't right. Sometimes, it was the approach. Sometimes, it was the concept. By diversifying your results and prioritizing in terms of focus on your vital few, you can be selective about your high risk bets. Your vital few results will cushion you when you stumble; alternatively, you can redirect your energy and re-establish momentum when something else just isn't working out. The opposite is to put all your eggs in one basket. The problem is that life has more than one basket. If you spend all your time in your career, then your relationships or body can go downhill. Too much time having too much fun will weaken your body or mind. The different buckets support each other and help improve your overall effectiveness. Yet when you have a good bet, not to go for it! Follow your passion, but use your portfolio to keep things in check and not lose sight of the bigger picture.

Strategy 8: Next Best Thing to Do

What's the next best thing to do? Believe it or not, the key difference in a lot of productivity systems boils down to answering that question. It's a great question to tackle because time is your most precious resource. You can't make more of it. You can only spend it more wisely. This is where all your outcomes, priorities, trade-offs, and focus meet.

The question can be more powerful than the answer, because there is no one answer. Instead, it's a quick check to help you course correct. You might already ask yourself in fuzzy or indirect ways. That's completely different than asking yourself such a pointed question at the start of your week, at the start of your day, or in the moment. Before you worry about whether you have the right answer, get in the habit of asking the question. Your mind is a powerful resource when you ask the right questions.

Strategy 9: Value Delivered over Backlog Burndown

Like the camel loaded with one too many straws on its back, your backlog can wear you down, even break you. Backlogs tend to be a laundry list of items that once were important, but time changes the value of things. Your backlog is an input for you, but you should never be a slave to it. Doing so will result in missed opportunities.

A Catalog of Potential Action

Instead of being backlog driven, think in terms of value delivered. You backlog is a catalog of potential action. You probably have more things to do than there is time in the day. That would be a problem if all things were equally important, right here, right now. Instead, each moment, each day, each week, you get to choose the most valuable things to do. This is where asking yourself what's the next best thing to do really comes into play. It might be an item in your backlog. It might not. How do you know? It's based on what you want to accomplish (your outcomes), how you want to maximize your impact, and what's valued. The key here is delivering value over backlog burndown.

Backlogs Rot with Time

Backlogs tend to have two problems. First, backlogs rot over time. The longer an item sits in a backlog, the better chance that it's time has come and gone, or that something else is more important now. The second common problem is they are often overly detailed plans. Thus was coined the saying, "A plan is a list of things that will never happen." It's better to elaborate and add detail when you're actually going to do something. Don't get bogged in details. Stick with tickler lists with just enough notes to feed into your decisions and to remind you what's important. Don't become a beast of burden to your backlog. Instead, let it serve you.

Value Is in the Eye of the Beholder

Always remember that value is in the eye of the beholder. Know who the customer is when you're working on something. Is it you for your personal learning? Is it for your boss? Get clarity on that first. If it's for not for you, you need to know whether what you're doing is considered above the line or below the line. Below the line is simply expected. Above the line is valued. Don't be surprised if you don't get a raving review when all you did was below the line work. At the same time, don't screw up great results by failing to meet basic expectations. Part of your success is how you manage expectations, with yourself and others.

Strategy 10: Make It a Project

If you want to get real results, make it a project. When you make something a project, you turn it into something more manageable. You give it a start and a finish. You can figure out the work involved. You can weigh the benefits of it against other things you might invest your life force in. For example, let's say you want to improve how you handle your email. Now you have something real to focus on or direct your energy towards. Giving it a name puts you in control. You now have a named thing that you can prioritize. You have something specific and you can experiment with the best ways to accomplish it. You now have a named thing that you can put on the backburner, associate actions to, or measure your results on. You can drive it from cradle to grave.

Chunk It Up

Based on my experience on many projects over many years and the experience of others, you're better off in the long run of doing many short projects over one long marathon. You build momentum. You get a fresh start. You can version your results. For example, you might do a short project to test your results. At the end of your project, you can evaluate your results. Not happy with your results? Maybe it's time for version two, if it's the next best thing for you to do. Remember that the power is in treating something as a project. Projects can vary dramatically in size. One effective way to right-size them is to do it by time. For example, you could have a day project, a weeklong project, a month-long project, a three-month project, a six-month project, etc. You want it long enough to get useful results and meaningful feedback, but not so long that it wears you down and you can't see the end in mind. Jump incremental hurdles over trying to scale a major wall.

Strategy 11: Have a Strong Week

Unless you've been deliberate about your schedule, there's a good chance you're spending a lot of your time on things that make you weak. The activities that drain you might be spread out all over the week. Some you may have control over, some you don't. Maybe you haven't even identified what makes you strong and what makes you weak?

Figure Out Your Weekly Strengths and Weaknesses

First, figure out the activities each week that make you weak and that make you strong. Pay special attention to what makes you weak. Things that make you weak are those which leave you feeling drained—not in a good way. You never look forward to them. Pay attention to what makes you strong. It may be things you enjoy, or it might not. Things that make you strong give you more energy when you perform them. Knowing yourself is a huge advantage over ignorance. This list is your insider's guide to improving your energy levels.

Consolidate and Compartmentalize Your Weaknesses

Next, fix your week. Don't let your weaknesses spring leaks in an otherwise potentially strong schedule. Whether you designed it on purpose or not, you already have a weekly schedule. This is your chance to create a strong week by design. Based on Peter Drucker's recommendations and what I've tested in practice, a good way to start is by pushing as much of the things that make you weak to Mondays and to the morning in your day. Compartmentalize them. By consolidating them and shoving them into timeboxes, you stop the energy leaks throughout your week. Why does this work? You use the strongest part of your day, to get over your major humps. Ideally, you line up things that make you strong right after to give you a boost. By structuring your days and week like this, you design your momentum. Otherwise, you either luck into weakness or luck into strength. Don't leave your success to luck. Know the keys and continuously work towards and refine them. The beauty of designing a week that supports you is you get to practice every week.

Strategy 12: Know Yourself

You can learn all the strategies in the world, but if you don't know your own patterns, there's a good chance they won't help. If you know your own patterns, strengths, and weaknesses, then you can choose and adopt more effective strategies. Here are some ways to know yourself in relation to personal productivity:

1. **Mindsets and Motivation.** If it's not working for you, change your mindset; this is one of the most powerful things you can do. For example, if you realize that you tend to be negative, test adopting a positive mindset for a month. If you have a fixed mindset (one which assumes that things are the way they are and you can't improve them), adopt instead a growth mindset where you test your ability to thrive and to learn. Rather than just think of things as natural talent, think of things in terms of skills waiting to be developed. This opens a lot of doors to you. Again, test it for a month to decide whether this is right for you.

2. **Metaphors.** You probably already represent your work to yourself in some way. Maybe you think of yourself as the lone cowboy. Maybe your work is like herding cats. Maybe you're Atlas with the world on your shoulders. However you are thinking of it, write these down. Are they helping you or working against you? One metaphor that helps me is thinking in terms of mastering my craft. Another is taking the bull by the horns. Think of metaphors that empower you and swap them out for the ones that make you weak.

3. **Personas.** You probably know whether you are a starter or a Finisher, a Maximizer or a Simplifier, a Thinker or a Doer, etc. Whenever there's work to do, think about which persona helps you best and put on that hat. Additionally, consider the opportunity to pair up with other personas. If you're a Finisher, then see if you can find a good Starter to help get you going.

4. **Introvert or Extrovert.** Introverts are more focused on internal ideas and you may prefer to work alone or in small groups. Extroverts on the other hand may want to work as part of larger teams or where there's more real-time communication. Know your pattern and set yourself up to keep your energy high. If you're an introvert, this means getting your alone time. If you're an extrovert, this means spending time with others.

5. **Strengths and Weaknesses.** You should know your strengths such as detail oriented or quick on your feet or great presentation

skills. You should know and respect your weaknesses. You should reduce your liabilities and invest more energy in growing your strengths over your weaknesses.

6. **Passions.** If you know your passions, you can make time to refuel. You can also find ways to work your passions into your current job. There's always a way, it's just a matter of degree.

7. **Fighting Perfectionism.** Most people have some trace of perfectionism. Some people have it more than others. Find ways to overcome your perfectionism, such as versioning your results and improving each time, and adopting beliefs such as perfection is a journey not a destination.

8. **Fighting Procrastination.** You know your patterns better than anybody. If you keep finding yourself procrastinating, one of the common problems is you're thinking too much and you talk yourself out of it. One quick solution is to simply start taking more action. Another issue is that most people think they have to talk themselves into doing something. The problem is that action comes before motivation. If you know this, then again, the trick is to take action and let motivation follow. Find ways to look forward to what you do, and work on way to reduce friction. Create more glide-paths for yourself.

9. **Linking to Good Feelings.** Know how to push your own buttons. Pay attention to what makes you feel good: certain memories, certain thoughts, certain songs. Think the thoughts that make you feel good, recall the memories that make you feel great, or play the songs that get you fired up when you need to link things to good feelings. To put it another way, if you whistle while you work, you might find new ways to enjoy old things.

10. **Compelling "Why."** Make sure you know why you do what you do. This is your simple most important carrot that you can use to help motivate yourself when the going gets tough. It's also your reminder and checkpoint to stay on track.

11. **Workspace Pattern.** Some people like to work with others. Some people like to work alone. Some people like to work on their own thing, but with other people. If you know this about yourself, see if you can arrange your projects to support your most effective work style. Otherwise, recognize the issues and ask friends and mentors for strategies that help you improve your effectiveness.

12. **Time.** Some people care a lot more about time than others. For example, they're always on time and they never miss deadlines. They are quick to set dates and meet them. Other people care a lot more about quality and actually taking their time. They often send belated birthday cards, are late to parties, and regularly miss deadlines. Others are somewhere in the middle. You should know which end of the spectrum you fall. If you tend to be scope and quality driven, test focusing more on time for a month. Set daily, weekly, monthly goals and bite off a little at a time. Focus on getting drafts or strawman or prototypes done over fit and finish. The key is to see what it feels like to do things on time and to trade perfection for timely results. One of the worst failure patterns I see time and again is this: "It will be done when it's done" and the recurring missed deadlines that inevitably follow. That just doesn't work in today's world. It's one of the toughest things to learn, but it's about finding a balance with sharing "good enough" sooner versus too little too late.

Strategy 13: Team Up

Pair up, team up, buddy up, whatever. Find somebody to complement your skills. If you're a Starter, pair with a Finisher. If you're a Maximizer, pair with a Simplifier. If you're a Thinker, pair with a Doer. This keeps momentum and you get the benefit of synergy.

I've seen a lot of people get stuck. For whatever reason, they hit an invisible wall. Pairing with the right person got them over it. Consider teaming up with somebody at work. Consider teaming up with somebody on something you want to learn. There's a lot of mentors in the world, you just need to know what you want and go for it. Most people that are good at something, like to share what they know. The trick is often finding and asking the right person.

Strategy 14: Factor Thinking from Doing

What do the most successful people that get results have in common? They don't second guess themselves every step of the way. They don't analyze everything while they do it. They decide and go.

Why is this such a big deal? This is how you avoid task saturation and shutting down. It's also how you avoid analysis paralysis. If you think your whole way through every step, you burn up your prefrontal cortex. That's the thoughtful part of your brain. If you find yourself constantly drained, there's a good chance you aren't taking enough breaks or you are interspersing too much thinking with your doing. This isn't about being mindless. It's about factoring your thought processes. For example, if you edit while you write, you slow yourself down and you wear yourself down. Instead, the recommendation is to write it out and then edit. The same holds true for brainstorming. You don't critique while you brainstorm. First, you brainstorm; then, you critique. Likewise, for task execution, you think; then, you execute. Basically, you do it; then, you review it and improve it.

There's another benefit to this approach. You can literally script your success. If you think through your actions up front, you can write the key actions to execute. If this is a routine that you'll perform regularly, you now have a script that you can improve. In fact, I call these improvement scripts. This is one of the secrets the Air Force uses to turn ordinary people into extraordinary pilots.

Strategy 15: Factor Practice from Performance

This is related to factoring thinking from doing, but in this case, it's being clear about whether you're practicing or you're performing. When you're practicing, it makes sense for you to go slower and be more thoughtful to get the routine down or learn a new technique. You might even be doing a dry run. When you're performing, you can't be second guessing yourself along the way. Simply perform.

Strategy 16: Measure Against Effectiveness

How do you judge a technique? Measure by what works. You can't argue with results. More importantly, measure against effectiveness. For something to be useful, it first needs to be effective. It needs to work. You can want it to work all you want, but you have to be honest with what you're getting. If it's not working change your approach. That's the key to success. Throw out what works in favor for what works. There are many ways to accomplishing something; the challenge, of course, is finding the right technique.

Strategy 17: Know What You're Getting

When you take actions, you produce results. Pay attention to what you're getting. This includes both qualitative and quantitative feedback. There are always clues.

The pitfall is to kid yourself when it counts. The quicker you have a good sense of how things are actually working out, the faster you can change your approach to something that might work better. Producing results is a constant exercise in course correction. Trust your intuition. If your mind says things are on track, but your gut says something is off, dig deeper. You might be picking up on something intuitively that you just haven't figured out how to rationalize yet. Always balance your intuition with your mind. Don't react to what you don't understand. As you ask better questions, you'll eventually figure out what you intuitively sensed. A simple way to use your intuition more when you're analyzing what you're getting is to ask, "What does my gut say?"

Strategy 18: Model the Best

One of the ways to find the best technique is to model from others or to find reference examples. Stand on the shoulders of giants. No matter what you're doing, chances are you're not the first. One of the worst mistakes people make is reinventing the wheel. "Best" is subjective and context dependent. What's important is that you meet your objectives in the most effective and efficient way you can. That's both the art and the science of results.

Leverage Your Heroes

You can also think of this as an exercise in impersonation. For example, you can ask yourself, "What would Einstein or da Vinci do in this scenario?" This is a great way to switch your thinking and gain new perspectives. This assumes that you know enough of the other person's thought patterns and behaviors to draw from. You'd be surprised how little it takes though to figure this out. You can gain a lot of insight into behaviors through "thin slicing," a concept introduced by Malcolm Gladwell in his book, *Blink: The Power of Thinking Without Thinking*. Thin slicing simply means extrapolating expectations about behavior by watching somebody in small periods of time.

Find the Mentors

When you look for mentors, find people that are getting the results you want. I know it sounds obvious, but I see a lot of people just ask smart people or just ask their friends. You want to find a few people that are succeeding where you want to succeed. They'll know what works and what doesn't work. They can save you a lot of time, especially by telling you which paths to avoid. You may have to tailor their guidance for your situation, but at least you aren't starting from scratch.

Strategy 19: Test Your Results

One useful metaphor for this is to "do a dry run." You don't always know what you're capable of. The fastest way to get some useful feedback is to test your results. Call it an experiment and see what you can do. Don't rely on your ability to predict what you can do; take action and get real feedback instead. One of the big surprises for people is when they believe they can't do something and they actually test their can'ts. Sometimes it works better to try to prove your right. If you really think you can't do something, prove it. There's a good chance you'll be surprised. Remember that what the mind can conceive, the body will achieve. You don't want to be the bottleneck to your own success. Lastly, testing your results early on is important so that you get a relative gauge of what you know, don't know and need to know next, as well as potential risks. As soon as you get some tangible feedback, you can start to make better estimates, you can start asking better questions, and you can start figuring out where the most valuable places are to spend your time. Don't be afraid to be wrong sometimes!

Strategy 20: Ask Better Questions

The right questions can dramatically improve your results. They can improve your efficiency and effectiveness. They can improve your state of mind. In contrast, the wrong questions can waste your time and put you in a deadlock. The right questions can save you from working on the wrong things, or using the wrong approach. They can get you out of a bind. If you know how to ask more effective questions, you can easily avoid deadlocks and keep forward momentum.

Ask Yourself Better Questions

Avoid asking yourself "Why" questions, such as "Why can't I do this?" You'll put yourself in a non-resourceful state and your mind will come up with reasons why you can't. Instead, ask more resourceful questions such as, "How can I solve this?" or, "How can I make the most of this?" or, "How can I improve this?" Your questions should support you, not disable you. If you get stuck in a loop when you ask yourself, "How can I solve this?" and you keep responding, "I don't know," switch the question and answer this instead: "Well, if you did know, how might you solve it?" I've used this many times to get myself and other people out of deadlocks. You'd be surprised how many people get stuck here, simply because they got stuck on needing a perfect answer instead of a potential path.

Ask the Right People

One of the fastest ways to waste your time is to ask the wrong people. Who knows more about which small businesses are working, an accountant who handles the taxes of many small businesses each year, or your get rich quick friend who saw the latest infomercial? You want to ask people with results. You want to ask people who are relevant to your scenario or problem. You want to ask people who are also capable of helping. You can save yourself a lot of wasted time simply by asking yourself if you're asking the right person. If you aren't sure, go ahead and start asking, but keep moving forward. One way to move forward is asking those who don't really know for somebody who does.

Solution-Focused Questions

I call empowering questions, "solution-focused questions." I think the name says a lot. It's about focusing on the solution, instead of dwelling on the problem. It's biased by design to help keep you from getting stuck in analysis paralysis and for taking action as quickly as possible. You'll learn more by doing and get better feedback. Asking solution-focused questions that are forward looking and optimistic will help you keep moving ahead as you face adversity and friction. They will be your greatest ally in terms of producing results.

Time, Cause, Effect, Meaning, and Action

Some of the best questions you can ask are pretty basic. You can ask questions about time, cause, effect, meaning, and action. For example, a time-based question would be "Is now the right time?" A question about cause would be "What's the root cause?" A question about effect would be "If we do this, what will be the impact?" A question about meaning would be "What does this mean?" You might ask a question about action such as, "Do we have the right people?" or, "What's the best thing to do?" One practical way I use this is when I have a meeting. One of the most important questions is "Are the right people here?" If not, there's no point in having the meeting. A few of the right questions can go a long way in improving your results.

Strategy 21: Enjoy the Process

Don't let the focus on results trump your approach. You have to enjoy the process, or you won't achieve sustainable results. This doesn't mean that every aspect along the way tickles you pink. What it means is that you feel the journey is worth it, and it's not just because of the destination. You become more along the way without sacrificing the basics along the way: like your health, your mind, your emotions, your relationships, and your fun.

Have a Metaphor

Sometimes enjoying the process is as simple as changing your mindset. "Working on your masterpiece" is an entirely different experience than just trying to get something done. Metaphors work wonders for helping you enjoy the process. Whether you see yourself as a craftsman, a mentor, an expert, or a novice can profoundly impact how much enjoyment you get along the way. This is also true for the metaphor you use for work. Is it a sprint? A marathon? An epic journey? An adventure? A SWAT mission?

One Pitch at a Time

The more the pressure is on, the more likely you are to watch the scoreboard. Pressure can help you improve your performance, but you need to focus on the right things. Instead of the scoreboard, focus on one pitch at a time. Trust that whatever you are doing at the moment is what you decided as your next best thing to do, and focus on it. You'll improve your performance. More importantly, you'll enjoy the process.

The beauty of this approach is it works instantly. Right now are you worrying about something you haven't finished? Or did you decide this was the next best thing to do and you're lost in the moment, asking yourself, how can you use this? All it takes is a simple shift in mindset to go from hating a task to savoring the moment. For example, if you decide to master your craft, then each session is a new opportunity to improve your efficiency and effectiveness. This sets you up for learning and growing. The opposite is doing your time and then wondering where your time went—one pitch at a time.

Find Your Passion

Where attention goes, energy flows. Energy is your fuel for results. One approach is to follow your passion. The other is to find your passion. Chances are that before you go looking somewhere else, you can find ways to enjoy what you do. One way to do this is to connect to your values. For example, when I lead my projects I turn them into epic adventures. I have value adventure, and I find that connecting to my values helps me find my passion in whatever I do.

Pace Yourself

Your pace can have a lot to do with your energy and enjoyment. Is it a marathon or a sprint? Is it a series of sprints? This is where knowing the system and knowing the cycle come into play. This is also where knowing yourself really pays off. You need to find the pace that best supports you. Sometimes, the turtle really does win the race. Other times, what you might just need is the thrill of a race with yourself or a race against time to really get it in gear and enjoy what you're doing. Fast can be fun and it can be furious. Slow can be a great way to savor the moments as you go. What's the key? Be deliberate about the pace you choose. It's helpful to work backwards from when you want the results. This can include important timing windows. You can then setup mini milestones.

Find the Lessons

There's always a lesson to be learned. When you don't get the results you expect, look for the lesson—that's where experience comes from if you choose to learn from it.

Strategy 22: Link It to Good Feelings

One of the important keys to enjoy the process is to link your routines and activities to good feelings. If you try to motivate yourself by promising rewards down the line, that's not very effective in the long run. It's actually important to link what you do to good feelings where possible. If you simply try to talk yourself into something, then all you end up with is a logical argument that's not very motivating. You get more leverage on yourself if you create an emotional connection. For example, let's say you don't like the pain of working out. One technique you can use is to play your favorite songs. You'll end up linking the workout to feeling good. Now you have your mind, body, and emotions working with you instead of against you.

Resistance Makes You Stronger

While the ideal scenario is you can make everything feel good, the reality is you can't. One thing that helps is to remember that resistance makes you stronger. When you lift weights, it may not feel good at the time, but you'll get stronger from the exercise. This holds true for when you're facing intellectual challenges as well. Ultimately, if you're on your path, resistance makes you stronger. What you have to watch out for is "pushing the weight sideways" (a phrase coined by my colleague Jason Taylor). What it means is that the resistance you're facing isn't actually helping. It's like somebody pushing the weight sideways while you're trying to work out.

Strategy 23: Make the Most of What You've Got

You'll end up in a lot of situations that aren't ideal. That's called life. Your ability to stand strong when tested will serve you in the long run.

Get in a Resourceful State

One of the best ways to make the most of any situation is to ask yourself, "How can I make the most of this situation?" This will put your mind in a more resourceful state.

Play to Your Strengths

Another way to make the most of what you've got is to play to your strengths. The simplest way to play to your strengths is to spend more time in your strengths, and less time in your weaknesses. While you can improve your weaknesses, you get more results by maximizing your strengths.

Strategy 24: Teach What You Need to Learn

One of the best ways to learn something is to teach it. It forces you to learn the information at a deeper level. Rather than just recognition, you work on your recall. You also get exposed to more questions and perspectives. Teaching requires you to burn info in at a deeper level. This requires sustained thinking and focus. One of the best forcing functions that to drive information home is simply the thought process of asking and answering questions. Of course, as you put the information into practice, you'll want to know it beyond the intellectual. Through repetition and practice you'll want to burn it at an emotional and physical level.

Strategy 25: Pave the Way Forward

If you think of yourself as a pathfinder, you can improve your results. Rather than stumble on results, pave a path towards it. When you find a path that works, you can improve the path by doing some simple things. For example, you can focus on reducing friction: walk your path end-to-end, identify your trouble spots, and then tune and prune the path to improve the results.

Make It Easy for You

Create a glide path for yourself. Create routines or checklists that support you. Once you create a script, you can evaluate its efficiency. Thinking on paper is powerful. You'll probably find ways to reduce the friction or find ways to enjoy the process more. You can share your script with others and ask for feedback on improving it. The creative replies may surprise you. If you treat what you do like a system, you can improve it systematically. Your system should support you, not the other way around.

Make It Easy for Others

Create a glide path for others. You can gauge the level of maturity of your system by how well you can either ramp other people up to do what you do or how easily you can hand over the reins. This is where your checklists, routines, and techniques come into play.

In Summary

- Familiarize yourself with the 25 strategies for getting results and draw from them as needed to help you turn the underlying principles into action.
- Use the strategies to help guide your tactics.
- Tailor and adapt the strategies to suit your scenarios and context.
- Test strategies to find what works.
- Mix and match strategies as appropriate.

Chapter 13 – Motivation

The first and best victory is to conquer self. —Plato, Greek Philosopher

In This Chapter

- Learn how to improve your motivation and self-discipline through a compelling "Why," vision, and outcomes.
- Learn the key pitfalls that work against your motivation.
- Learn the key factors that influence your motivation.

Motivation is the "Why" behind the goal. It's your little engine that says you can, when the rest of you says you can't. It's also the same force that on a good day can help you move mountains. Motivation is a life-long skill that you can improve through self-awareness and proven strategies. **The better you know your own drivers and levers, the more effective you'll be at getting the results you want in your life.**

Then there's self-discipline: the ability to correct your behavior. (Self-discipline is simply correcting or regulating your behavior for the sake of improvement. Will is based on thinking and reason to create action. Motivation is rooted in emotion.) It helps you get back on course when you fall off your path. When inclined to do otherwise, self-discipline helps you do the right thing in the moment for your long-term benefit. According to Stephen Covey, "Only the disciplined are truly free. The undisciplined are slaves to moods, appetites, and passions." **Self-discipline is a muscle that gets stronger the more you flex it.**

Motivation and self-discipline work hand in hand. Motivation can be your initial inspiration. Lose your initial inspiration and self-discipline keeps you going. But to commit to self-discipline, it's your initial motivation that convinces you it's worth it.

One of the most important things I realized is that **motivation can come from your thoughts, feelings, or your body.** You might think yourself into something. You might feel motivated, perhaps inspired by your thoughts. Or your body might motivate you, as a seasoned runner feels the urge to go running. On the other hand, self-discipline is only ever driven from your thinking. Success reinforces your self-discipline. **The most important point about self-discipline is that you don't talk yourself into it, it's a decision.** You simply decide. And how do you decide? Your motivation.

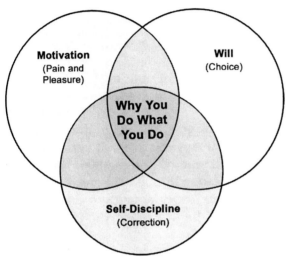

Figure 13.1
Why You Do What You Do

Motivational Quotes

Quotes reflect the wisdom of the ages. Some people have an amazing way with words. The right quote can lift you up and get you back on track when you need it. Great wordsmiths have given us powerful perspectives on motivation and self-discipline. Here are a handful of my favorite quotes:

- *You don't overcome challenges by making them smaller but by making yourself bigger.* —John C. Maxwell
- *Fall seven times. Stand up eight.* —Japanese Proverb
- *It's not whether you get knocked down, it's whether you get up.* — Vince Lombardi
- *The price of discipline is always less than the pain of regret.* —Nido Qubein

- *Motivation is the fuel necessary to keep the human engine running.* —Zig Ziglar
- *Happiness comes when you believe in what you are doing, know what you are doing, and love what you are doing.* —Brian Tracy

Pain and Pleasure

Pain and pleasure are the keys to motivation. When you really want something, you'll find a way. Likewise, when you really want to avoid something, you'll find a way. You'll go further out of your way to avoid pain than gain pleasure. It's a survival mechanism. When your basic needs are unmet, you feel pain. That pain drives you to survive. Once your basic needs are met, you seek to thrive. This includes reducing pain, while seeking pleasure.

Pleasure

You can't always talk yourself into liking something. You have to pay attention to your emotional response. For example, you might know that working out is good for you and you would think that should be enough to enjoy it. The problem is that's only at the intellectual level. Physically, you might feel a lot of pain. One common technique is to listen to your favorite songs. Listening to your favorite songs or power songs helps you link pleasure.

Pain

If there's something you want to do, but won't, then you've associated more pain with doing it than not doing it. Whether it's the fear of rejection or the fear of failure, it's pain. The memory of past pain and anticipation of future pain are also key aspects. In-the-now pain can make you stop, but usually it's rooted in the past or future (i.e., in your head). Whether the pain is real or imagined and whether it's physical, emotional, or mental, it's still pain. It could be a timing issue. Your perceived pain now might outweigh your perceived pleasure down the line. If there's something you keep doing, but logically it doesn't make sense, you're either getting pleasure from it or avoiding pain. Gradually, you slide towards things that feel good and away from things that don't. This is why you might talk yourself into working out, but if you don't find a way to enjoy it, it's easy to slide out of it.

Compelling "Why," Vision, and Outcomes

Your compelling "Why," vision, and outcomes support you on your path to results. If you want to make something happen, have a compelling "Why." Make it your cause. A compelling vision is a scene you can easily conjure with the end in mind—it's how you imagine the world will be different. A good test is whether you can draw your vision. It's like having a finish line. The outcomes are the results you will experience. You can think of your vision as the future picture, and your outcomes as the details or highlights of the scene.

Compelling "Why"

Why are you doing this? If you don't have a reason you feel strongly about, chances you may give up in the face of resistance. Have a compelling "Why" to help you get back up if you get knocked down. It's your single best tool to keep you going. Whenever you start out on a path, you might have a fuzzy picture of the end in mind. Your "Why" will help guide you through. One common reason people give up on their goals is that the why wasn't important enough. They didn't emotionally connect with it. It might have looked good on paper, but it wasn't compelling. Additionally, your compelling "Why" may lead to a compelling vision. Sometimes it's easy, or it may take some work. You may have to get creative. Difficulty discovering a compelling "Why" may be an indicator that there's something else you'd rather spend your time on.

Compelling Vision

It's easier to stay motivated if you see the end in mind. A vision of the end in mind, especially a compelling one, is a tool to help you stay the course. Sometimes your compelling vision creates a compelling "Why." If you really like the end in mind, the why becomes obvious and lets you latch onto it. A friend of mine used a movie technique to finish an Iron Man competition. He visualized watching himself on the screen of his favorite theater. In his mental movie he would see himself running his upcoming race. He added a lot of details to make it vivid: his film is shot high from a helicopter with his favorite announcers calling out his name as he crosses the finish line. He attributes visualizing his success as a movie to his actual success in the race.

Compelling Outcomes

An outcome is the end result. Tasks and activities are the means to get there. Some outcomes are more valuable than others. Value is in the eye of the beholder; that's why, at work, you line up value against business objectives and the culture of your tribe, team, or group (i.e., know what the group values). Think of outcomes as sets of results you want to achieve. Don't settle for a fuzzy notion of results; make it as precise as possible. Imagine results that you can see, hear, feel, and touch.

10 Pitfalls of Motivation

There are many common myths and some bad practices that take away your motivation. Another key is to know your own patterns and anti-patterns. Anti-patterns are simply bad patterns, or examples of how not to do things. Understanding all these pitfalls helps avoid them.

1. **Waiting for Inspiration.** Don't wait. Motivation follows action. Imagine if athletes only practiced on days they felt inspired. The rigor of their routines gives them their inspiration. Some days are better than others, but when inspiration happens they're ready to act on it. Develop routines that are easy to stick with and that give you chances to grow your skill and be your best. The more you practice, the more your skills evolve from intellectual, to emotional, until they are finally integrated into your body. You must set yourself up for flow opportunities or being "in the zone" to happen.

2. **Analysis Paralysis.** Don't fall into the trap of analysis paralysis. It's a common way to get yourself stuck, spending too much time on the problem instead of the solution. If you're spending 80 percent of your time mulling on the problem and only 20 percent working on the solution, then flip it. Few problems can withstand sustained action that builds momentum and confidence.

3. **Perfectionism.** Don't let perfection get in the way of good enough. Perfection comes in many forms. You might think that you're not good enough or smart enough. You might think the work is not good enough. One way to fight perfectionism is to call the work an experiment. Another way is to work one version at a time. For example, do a first version of the work as a rough cut,

then clean it up in the next version, and so on, improving each time. Timeboxing is another way to help fight perfectionism. By giving yourself time limits, you do your best with the time you have. Give your best and focus on the learning.

4. **Churning.** It's easy to burn yourself out if you continually go round and round on a problem without making progress or if find yourself solving the same or similar problems repeatedly. Excitement and energy comes from learning and growing, not spinning your wheels. When you are stuck, try a new approach; see if you can redefine the problem, tackle one piece of it, or find a mentor. Be careful; it's important that you also recognize the difference between churning and a problem that just takes time. Some problems require chipping away at the stone; it may not seem like much, but your constant action gradually wears it down, until finally you breakthrough.

5. **Lack of Boundaries.** Have you noticed when you push yourself past your limits you lose energy fast? This could be anything from staying up too late, to waiting too long to eat, to over-sustained thinking. Set limits and use them to keep yourself fresh.

6. **Choosing the Wrong Motivation.** Don't let the wrong motivation take you off track. Remember that goals are a vehicle, a means to an end. The power of goals is that you grow while you stretch to reach them. Be careful what you wish for, because you just might get it. Periodically check your direction against where you want to be. Don't invest your time, energy, and resources only to find out your ladder was up against the wrong wall.

7. **Overwhelming Yourself.** Don't bite off more than you can chew. Instead, take smaller bites and finish faster. This builds momentum. Don't create your own walls that you can't scale by overloading yourself. A simple way to break this pattern is to start simple and achieve success. Incremental success becomes a habit.

8. **Beating Yourself Up.** Don't burden yourself with past defeats. Pick yourself up when you fail—it's OK. Be wary of "should" thinking, another easy trap to fall into. Instead, focus on the vital things toward achieving your best results.

9. **Watching the Scoreboard.** It's good to know the score, but don't let that be your focus. Your focus should be on one pitch at a time. When you focus on the task at hand, giving it your best, you set yourself up for improved performance. Focusing on the

scoreboard is a way to create anxiety without improving. Focus on your current level of play, and take the scoreboard as feedback. Use it to improve, but don't let it become a distraction.

10. **Death by a Thousand Paper Cuts.** Friction in your daily routines builds up over time. All this friction adds up, slowing you down, and wasting precious mental energy. These little things stop people far more often than larger forces, yet usually go unseen. At first you might not notice any friction in your initial burst of enthusiasm and inspiration. But inspired action only takes you so far. By noticing friction (even minor ones) early on, you can nip it in the bud while you still have momentum. Set yourself up for success by creating glide-paths for your most important routines. Focus on the Hot Spots in your routines to reduce a little friction each day. This adds up to great improvement over time.

10 Key Strategies for Motivation

When the problem is motivation, you need some time-tested tools to help you get going. Here are ten key strategies for motivation:

1. **See the End in Mind.** You need to know when you're done as well as what good results look like. You might not have the "perfect" map from point A to point B, but at least know your destination. Don't just vaguely imagine it—see it in your mind's eye. A good test is if you can draw your vision or concisely tell others what you're trying to accomplish. It's easier to stay the course when you can see the finish line. And it's also easier to keep going when know that you will like where you're going. Course corrections are easier and more accurate when you know your progress toward your destination.

2. **Make It Meaningful.** Having a purpose, a compelling one, is key to driving results. Sometimes it's as simple as redefining your purpose when your original purpose isn't working. Use the right metaphor. Frame it in a compelling way. Redefine it. Is it a mountain or a molehill? Are you on a mission? Sometimes all it takes is the right emotional picture word to give new meaning to your activity.

3. **Use Pain and Pleasure to Get Leverage.** Make it painful not to do it. Make it pleasurable to do it. Find a way to enjoy it. Rely on passion and in finding ways to enjoy doing what's good for you, not on discipline. Link tasks to pleasure. Change how you

feel about the stuff you do. Don't just assume you'll automatically like something over time, ensure it will happen. You can help it along by finding a more compelling reason or associating fun things, such as by playing your favorite songs.

4. **Master Self-Discipline.** Flex your self-discipline muscles. Some things are a trade-off: pay now or pay later. Self-discipline is often about trading away pleasure now (or even accepting some pain) for pleasing results later. Make resistance your friend—it makes you stronger.

5. **Make It a Routine.** Instead of discipline, use routine. You don't have to make yourself work too hard every time. Use checklists to improve. Focus on the learning. Master your craft. Bootstrap your routines by creating glide paths or simple ways to start.

6. **Set Boundaries.** Set a quota. Use timeboxes to limit the amount you do or to create time for short burst work. You can also use time boundaries to limit or compartmentalize pain. For example, if you have a bunch of activities that drain you, consolidate and batch them for an hour in the morning to get them out of the way. Another part to setting boundaries is having a fixed time for eating, sleeping, and working out—this is an extremely common success pattern. The sum of establishing these three routines is more than the parts because these three activities support each other. Having a routine for them helps you learn your energy patterns; your body also learns what to expect. For example, what you think is a motivation issue may really be a lack of sleep. Sometimes, it's simply because you don't eat at regular intervals that you lose energy. Working out often helps people sleep better and eat better.

7. **Build Momentum.** Set Incremental hurdles. Success builds momentum. One of the simplest ways to get into this pattern is to start with something simple that will lead to success. Incremental success becomes a habit.

8. **Take Action.** Motivation usually follows action, not the other way around. You'll also find that if you put in the hours, you'll have more chances for inspiration. Take full advantage of those inspirations when they occur.

9. **Reward Effort Over Performance.** You can control your effort, but not results. So focus on rewarding the effort and performance will follow in time. By focusing on what you control, you teach yourself to consistently give your best, independent of the

outcome. This raises your level of skill and sets you up for more positive outcomes.

10. **Team Up.** One of the most effective ways to find motivation is to team up with somebody. Find somebody who complements your strengths. If you're a Starter, find a Finisher. If you're a Maximizer (somebody who goes for completeness), find a Simplifier (somebody who simplifies). If you can, find somebody who's been there or done that before. Their experience can save you a lot of wasted time or energy. They can benefit honing their skill and leveraging experience, while learning something new along the way. You need to make it mutually beneficial to sustain it.

Self-Awareness is Your Best Strategy

Self-awareness is your best strategy for motivation. You need to know what makes you tick. You gain this self-knowledge through reflection, asking the right questions, and paying attention to your patterns. The more you know yourself, the better you can drive your own results. Observe which techniques work for you and which don't. For example

- *Do you like to work alone or with others?*
- *Does your encouragement come from internal or external factors?*
- *Do you know how to switch hats to switch your mindsets?*
- *Do you know your energy drains and your catalysts?*
- *Do you know how to use more meaningful metaphors?*

20 Key Factors for Motivation

What you don't know *can* hurt you, or at least work against you. While the simple model of motivation is based on pain and pleasure, you can master motivation by understanding what influences it.

I've outlined twenty key factors that can unleash a more motivated you. Some of these you can control more than others, but total awareness is critical. Paying attention to these factors sheds light on what is and isn't working for you in various scenarios. You have to know what you're looking for in order to see it. Use these factors as a new lens for uncovering what might be blocking you right now, or even over a lifetime. You need to experiment and learn what works best for you. Knowledge truly becomes power when applied to motivation. Here are the factors:

1. **Pain and Pleasure.** A simple model to think of motivation is pain and pleasure. We move towards pleasure and away from pain. Pain avoidance usually trumps pleasure seeking.

2. **Needs.** You must satisfy your basic needs before moving up the stack. In other words, you'll do more to get food and shelter before seeking out higher level goals.

3. **Intrinsic and Extrinsic Motivation.** Intrinsic motivation is how you motivate yourself by your thoughts, feelings and self-talk. For example, your reward might be the satisfaction of a job well done. Extrinsic motivations are external carrots and sticks, such as praise, money, or fear of punishment. For sustainable results, try to link things to intrinsic motivation and values.

4. **Attribution.** Do you attribute your success to things you control and your competency, or do you think it's beyond your control and just luck?

5. **Competence vs. Chance.** If you attribute your success to things you control, you'll prefer work based on your own competence. If you attribute your success to external factors, you'll prefer work that's based on competence and chance.

6. **Values.** The more you value something, the more motivated you will be to achieve it. You cannot be motivated by something you don't value.

7. **Passion.** Passion is your inner fire and the best fuel to get results. You can either chase the passion you know or find passion in what you already do. Knowing your preferences, strengths, and skills, helps to find your passion. You often have to look for the passion, but also know when it just isn't there and move on.

8. **Resistance.** Resistance makes you stronger. But too much can also demotivate you if it creates too much pain or stops you in your tracks. When you workout, knowing that the resistance is making you stronger enables you to enjoy the pain or at least tolerate it better.

9. **Mindsets and Metaphors.** The mindsets and metaphors you choose are the filters that shape your thoughts, feelings, and behaviors. For example, do you feel more motivated when you're on a "quest" or just doing the "daily grind"? Are you "mastering your craft" or just "putting in your time"? Are you "standing strong when tested" or just getting "beat down"?

10. **Thoughts.** Your thoughts create your feelings. This is why your self-talk or how you visualize something can either motivate or demotivate you.

11. **Feelings.** If you enjoy how something feels, you'll do it more. If you don't like how it feels, you'll do it less. You might be aware of how you feel or you might not even notice it. It's tough to keep doing something if it doesn't make you feel good either in the moment, or if you can't imagine the benefit in the future, or if you don't value the long-term benefit. Link things to good feelings for sustainable results.

12. **Body.** Your body can help you or work against you in terms of motivation. The three key activities that support each other are eating, sleeping, and exercise. One of the non-obvious threats to motivation is a lack of sleep. If you're not at your best, test your sleep patterns by sleeping different durations and noticing the impact. If you want something badly enough, your passion can overrule your body, but that's not sustainable. On the flip side, you can eat right, sleep right, and be in great shape, but without passion, you might not feel very motivated. Here's the surprise— action can come before motivation, and you're more likely to take action when you're body has the power it needs.

13. **People.** Do the people you spend your time with usually catalyze or drain you? Pay attention to the people and interactions that give you energy and take it away. Consider changing the people or changing how you interact.

14. **Tasks.** Do the tasks you work on catalyze or drain you? Do you look forward to them or drag your feet? Pay attention to the tasks you work on. Some will make you strong, while others will make you weak. Consider change the tasks or changing your attitude about the task.

15. **Workspace.** If you have a place for things and things in their place, your mind is freed up for better things. Give yourself a glide path for results by reducing little frictions that get in your way.

16. **Work Style.** Most people have a preference, but might not be aware of it, unless you think about it or experiment. There are three basic patterns: (1) you only like to work on your own thing; (2) you like to work on shared tasks as part of a group; or (3) you like to work on your own thing, but within a group. Find your best fit and try to work within that style. Don't accept work you will have to do in a style you aren't well suited for.

17. **Culture.** Culture is the shared values of a group. It's what they value by actions, not by words. For example, you might value results over process, but the culture at work might value process over results. Work that isn't valued will be difficult to get motivated for if you are externally driven. If your motivation is internally driven, it's less of a problem, but it's still an issue for you. Ideally, work within a culture that matches your values.

18. **Introverted vs. Extroverted.** If you're introverted, you prefer to think first and then act. You derive most of your energy inwardly from ideas and concepts. You likely prefer work you can do alone that requires concentration. In contrast, if you're extroverted, you probably prefer to act first and think later. You draw energy largely from other people or from things. Your motivation mostly comes from other people.

19. **Short-term View and Long-term View.** Some people have an easier time trading long-term gain for short-term pain than others who demand immediate gratification. Ideally, learn to master both. Work at finding ways to make things more enjoyable in the present and so you don't depend purely on a long-term. Find ways to work for the long-term where slow and steady wins the race.

20. **Skill Variety, Task Identity, and Task Significance.** Consider the meaningfulness of your work. Skill variety is the range of skills you need to perform your task. Task identity is the notion of a task as a whole, identifiable unit of work. Task significance is about how much the task means to others. These three factors often influence your motivation and ultimate satisfaction in a task.

In Summary

- Know your own drivers and levers; the better you know them, the more effective you'll be.
- Practice self-discipline; it's a muscle that gets stronger the more you flex it.
- Be aware of your thoughts, your feelings, and your body—it's where motivation comes from.
- Have a compelling vision of the end in mind.
- Have a compelling "Why" to help remind you of your mission and deal with resistance.
- Know the key pitfalls of motivation so you can avoid them.

- Know the key strategies for motivation so that you can motivate yourself more effectively.
- Know the key factors for motivation so that you can troubleshoot motivation issues more effectively, as well as use the right tool for the job.

Chapter 14 – Mindsets and Metaphors

Many people die at twenty five and aren't buried until they are seventy five. —Benjamin Franklin

In This Chapter

- Learn how to use mindsets and metaphors to improve your motivation.
- Learn how to effectively change your mindsets to improve your effectiveness in any situation.
- Learn how to make the most of luck.

This chapter shows you how to make the most of your mindsets and metaphors. The key to inspired action is using powerful imagery to invoke your emotions. World-class athletes use metaphors, visualizations, and winning mindsets to produce powerful results—you can too. You can easily change your mindset by asking different questions or "switching hats."

This chapter also helps you know the impact of personality type, focus, and attribution. Your personality type influences your motivation. For example, introverts tend to get energy when they're alone, while extroverts get their energy when they're with others. Where you put your focus (such as on yourself or others; on the situation; or in the past, present, or future) shapes your thinking, feeling, and doing.

A mindset is a mental attitude. It shapes your actions and your thoughts, as well as how you perceive and respond to events. A common example is whether you see the glass "half empty" or "half full." Your mindset can quickly change what you think, feel, and do. The irony of a mindset is that sometimes you don't know that you're stuck in one until you step out or adopt a different mindset. The trick is knowing how to switch mindsets. While there are lots of ways to change your mindset, I've found these to be the most effective ways: changing your questions, changing your metaphors, or changing the questions you ask yourself. Asking "What's wrong with this picture?" is completely different than asking "What's right?" In *It's a Wonderful*

Life, the main character, George Bailey, played by Jimmy Stewart, focuses on what's wrong with his life, until an angel who needs his wings shows him what's right with it. He realizes he's actually had a wonderful life.

Metaphors can be enabling or disabling. One of my most effective mentors taught me to think of metaphors as emotional picture words. With the right metaphor, you can inspire yourself to action. With the wrong metaphors you can quickly create a dark cloud that consumes you. When I work on big projects that need to make big impact, I think of it as an "epic adventure." This inspires me and the team to bold action. A colleague said he thinks of me as the director of blockbusters, so metaphors have an impact on how you see yourself and how others see you, too. When I think of stages in life, I think of boy, warrior, king, and sage. During my warrior years, I push myself to my limits, give my best where I have my best to give, and I mentor others. In fact, I like the mentor metaphor over guru. Another metaphor that helps me on projects is knowing whether I'm the quarterback or the coach, and when I'm not the quarterback, I need a quarterback I trust. Bruce Lee considered himself first and foremost a fighter and this metaphor shaped his life. Here is a simple, empowering metaphor we can all use: "You're the director of your life."

Whether life is a bowl of cherries and you get the pits, or the world is your oyster and you look for the pearls, you decide. In *The Last Lecture*, Randy Pausch taught us to choose whether we spring through life like Tigger, or mope through each day like Eeyore. Choosing your mindset and metaphors is one of the most powerful things you can do to shape your every day experience, and ultimately your life.

3 Mindsets that Support You

Your mindset can work either for you or against you; it either supports you or drags you down. Being cognizant of your mindset, you can ensure that you're focusing your energies on the right things—finding a way forward rather than just throwing more roadblocks in the way. The three mindsets that support you are

1. Abundance mindset
2. Positive mindset
3. Growth mindset

Adopt an Abundance Mindset over a Scarcity Mindset

Covey and others teach us to think in terms of abundance and avoid a scarcity mindset which can limit our ability to think in terms of possibilities. With an abundance mindset, you start with the assumption that there's more space and more resources than what you might see by default. You find a way to create more opportunities. You expand solutions to be inclusive of your ideas as well as others. Rather than fight turf wars, you create a larger space. Rather than fight for resources, you find more. When you operate from a scarcity mentality, you operate in survival mode and focus on threats and competition instead of opportunities and collaboration. While you can spend your energy competing, you can also spend it creating more alternatives, expanding opportunities, and finding abundance.

Adopt a Positive Mindset over a Negative Mindset

We need to be able to see what's right with a situation. We need to see the opportunities and the upside of things, and not get limited by our own negativity or the negativity of others. With a negative mindset, we quickly focus on what's wrong with the situation, finding flaws at every turn. While the negative mindset can be helpful in some situations, we need to be able to switch out of it. This doesn't mean you should avoid looking for flaws or stop using your critical thinking when evaluating ideas. It does mean spending more time finding solutions than finding problems. Find a way forward; avoid falling into a pattern of getting dragged down and stuck by your own pessimism.

Adopt a Growth Mindset over a Fixed Mindset

Swap out a fixed mindset with a growth mindset. If you have a fixed mindset, you attribute results to innate ability and discount learning. You think people are naturally good at what they do—they either have it or they don't. Rather than seeing the potential to shape things or grow your abilities over time, you see a static, unchanging, fixed world.

A growth mindset is a learning mindset. It's the belief that you can improve at whatever you do through the right training—it's believing in yourself and your own potential. And yes, you can teach an old dog new tricks. Here are some ways to adopt a growth mindset over a fixed mindset:

1. **Call it an "experiment."** This sounds like a trivial frame game, but I see it work for myself and others.
2. **Treat perfection as a path, not a destination.** If you're a perfectionist—like I was ... er, *am* ... er ... still fighting it—you know what I mean.
3. **Use little improvements over time.** Focus on little improvements and distinctions over time, versus instant success. It's consistent action over time that produces the greatest results. You're probably a master of your craft, whatever it is you do each day, every day. John Wooden focused his team on continuous, individual improvement and created the best winning team in history.
4. **Remind yourself you're growing or dying.** You're either climbing or sliding; there's no in-between (and the slide down is faster than the climb up!).
5. **Try again.** If at first you don't succeed, don't just give up. Remember folks like Thomas Edison who "failed" many, many times before finding "success"—it's a part of innovation.
6. **Focus on lessons over failures.** Remind yourself there are no failures—only lessons: one more way how "not" to do something.
7. **Fail fast.** The faster you "fail," the faster you learn.
8. **Don't take yourself or life too seriously.** If you take yourself too seriously, you'll never get out alive!
9. **Learn to bounce back.** It's not that you don't get knocked down; it's that you get back up.
10. **Give yourself time.** A lot of times the difference between results is time. If you only chase instant successes, you miss out on

opportunities. Walk, crawl, run. Or, if you're like me, sprint and sprint again.

11. **Start with something small.** Build momentum. Jumping an incremental set of hurdles is easier than scaling a giant wall.

12. **Build on what you know.** No matter where you are or what you do, you take yourself with you. Bring your game wherever you go.

13. **Learn to like what growth feels like.** I used to hate the pain of my workouts. Now, I know that's what growth feels like. The better I got at some things, the more I hated how awkward I was at some new things. Now I like awkward and new things. It's growth.

14. **Find a mentor and coach.** It doesn't have to be official. Find somebody who's great at what you want to learn. Most people like sharing how they got good at what they do. It's their pride and joy. I used to wonder where the "mentors" are. Then, I realized they're all around me every day.

15. **Have a learning approach.** Timeboxes, little improvements at a time, and focus go a long way for results. For me, I use 30 Day Improvement Sprints.

How to Change Mindsets

There are a few ways to change your mindsets:

1. **Ask yourself a different set of questions.** Asking yourself how you can make the most of the situation or how can you thrive instead of survive is a very different set of questions than asking yourself, "Why me?" or, "What's the use in trying?"

2. **Adopt a different set of assumptions.** For example, rather than assume there's not enough, assume there's more than enough and you just need to find it. Keep in mind that you should always test your assumptions, but adopting a different set of assumptions can help you reach different conclusions you might not otherwise explore.

3. **Adopt a different set of metaphors.** For example, rather than life as a tragedy, you could see life as a dramedy, complete with drama and comedy.

4. **Wear a different hat.** Similar to a metaphor, you can change your mindset by changing your hat.

Switching Hats

Have you ever put on your thinking cap? That's the idea here. Have a set of imaginary hats where each one represents a different mindset. Simply put on your hat when you need it. Wearing a hat can put you in a certain mindset and reduce conflict that you might normally feel trying to manage several different opposing viewpoints. This gets in the way of energy moving and forward progress. The key is using the right hats for the right situations. When you're in execution mode, you don't want to be wearing the analysis hat or the fear hat. You want the action hat. When you're in a highly political setting, the kick arse or action hat can get you in trouble if not using the political hat first.

Example Hats

Here are some example hats you might put on:

Table 14.1 Example Hats for Results

Hat	Description
Solution Engineer	When you have a puzzle to solve, put on your solution engineering hat to leverage your most resourceful self.
Explorer	When you need to learn new information, put on your explorer hat. Make it a game of exploring the new terrain.
Thinker	When you know you need your focus and concentration, put on your thinker hat.
Doer	To break yourself out of analysis paralysis, put on your doer hat and start taking action.

When I have to get serious results, I wear this hat: my "kick arse and take names" hat. Although I can just imagine wearing this hat, I actually have a hat that I use for this occasion; it truly is a power hat.

How to Switch Gears Using Your Hats

There are a few things to keep in mind that will help you effectively switch gears using hats:

1. **Have a set of hats that serve you.** Sometimes you need to do more thinking, other times more action.

2. **Remember the feeling.** One quick way to put your hat on is simply remember the feeling. Remembering how you felt when you were in a certain mode? You can restore the power of that moment in an instant.
3. **Experiment.** When your hat isn't working, swap it out with one that does. Don't be afraid to try out new hats to add to your repertoire.

If you're not into hats, you can always use your favorite song or mood music. It's whatever you can use to help you switch gears effectively. For example, one of my favorite songs is "Crazy Train" by Ozzy Osbourne. It's a power song for me. It was my wrestling team's theme song and it always got me pumped.

Personality Types and Motivation

There's a link between personality types and motivation. If you know your preferences, you can choose situations, approaches, and types of work that suit you better. Awareness is your friend. Here are some key distinctions between the personality types:

Thinking vs. Feeling

Thinking types are interested in systems, structures, and patterns. Feeling types are interested in people and their feelings.

Introverted vs. Extroverted

Introverts are directed towards the subjective world or their internal representation of ideas and values. Extroverts are directed towards the external, objective world.

Summary of Key Preferences by Personality Type

The following table presents a summary of key preferences for the different personality types as it relates to motivation:

Table 14.2 Summary of Preferences by Personality Type

Preference	Description
Introverted Thinking	Preference for task and process. Wants the details. Likes routines. Likes goals and tasks.
Introverted Feeling	Likes to help. Wants to be involved in decisions. Prefers a self-pace.
Extroverted Thinking	Preference for task and results.
Extroverted Feeling	Doesn't enjoy working alone. Doesn't like routine. Doesn't want the details.

Where to Put Your Focus

Focus is whatever you're thinking about. Depending on what you focus on, you can lift yourself up or put yourself down. Direct your focus to get in a more resourceful state. To change your focus, change the questions you ask yourself. If you find yourself stuck, try changing your focus from the result to the task, or from your competence to the value of the task, etc. Here are some examples of where you can put your focus:

- The task
- The value of the task
- How you perform the task
- Your competence
- Your performance
- The result
- The lesson

Past, Present, or Future

Shifting tense is an incredibly effective way to improve your motivation. You may not be aware of it, but you probably already use the past, present, and future to lift yourself up or bring yourself down. For example, remember a time in your life when you gave your best and you felt your strongest; simply by remembering one of your past, best experiences, you can invigorate yourself. In contrast, if you dwell on a past mistake, you can bring yourself down; instead, try shifting to future possibilities. Rather than ask yourself why you messed up, ask yourself how you can make the best of the situation. You can use the future to imagine exciting possibilities. Sometimes, however, the future might seem daunting or demanding. In that case, you can switch your focus to the present. Focus on the task at hand or one day at a time. Keep a few of your best memories on hand to remind yourself that you can always surprise yourself or that you can make things happen. If you must dwell, then dwell on your successes, not your past mistakes. You'll be most successful when you can choose the right tense to focus on to improve your effectiveness for your current scenario.

Learned Helplessness

Dr. Martin Seligman teaches us that learned helplessness is when you automatically think that there's nothing you can do that can make a difference, even though you can. It happens over a serious of experiences. It happens when you make a problem personal, permanent, and pervasive. For example, you're making the problem personal if you ask, "Why does this always happen to me?" This is why framing your challenges with the right mindset is so important.

Permanent, Personal, and Pervasive

Seligman teaches optimism as a skill. One of the lessons from Seligman is his frame for how we explain misfortunes: permanent, personal, and pervasive. Here's a summary of each dimension:

Table 14.3 Permanent, Personal, and Pervasive

Category	Description
Personal	You make the problem personal. You see the problem as something about you.
Permanent	You make the problem permanent. Rather than see the problem as something that will change over time, you see it as unchanging.
Pervasive	You make the problem pervasive. You generalize the problem and it permeates into other areas of your life, beyond the immediate concern.

When you're in the thick of things, it's easy to see problems as personal, permanent, and pervasive. The trick is to step out of your problems and logic your way through them. Simply by knowing that looking at problems through these lenses (permanent, personal, and pervasive) can lead to learned helplessness, can be enough to help you challenge your perspective. The beauty of these lenses is simply by knowing what they are and the issues they create can help you get more mindful and be more thoughtful about how you see the world.

Temporary, Situational, and Specific

How do you combat learned helplessness? You might be too close to the problems. Get perspective on the problems and don't fall into automatic thinking. By default, you might see problems as personal, permanent, and pervasive. By design, you can learn to test additional lenses. For example, when you look at problems, you can think of them as temporary (nothing is permanent), situational (it's not about you), and specific (don't generalize or blow it out of proportion). How do you know which lens to use? Let feedback and results be your guide. It's about paying attention to what you're getting and testing your results. You might have some skills to build or some flaws to fix, but you might be an unfair critic. The key is to move from critic to coach and step out of the situation and get a more objective perspective. Another key is to measure against effectiveness.

Solution-Focused Questions

Instead of problem-focused questions, ask yourself solution-focused questions. A problem-focused question would be "Why does this always happen to me?" A solution-focused question would be "What's the solution; what can I do to fix this?" Solution-focused questions help find a way forward. They put your mind in a more resourceful state.

Examples of Solution-Focused Questions

Here are examples of solution-focused questions:

- *What's the best I can do for this situation?*
- *If nothing were to ever to change, what's the one quality or skill I need to truly enjoy this?*

- *How can I make the most of it?*
- *How can I respond to the challenge?*
- *If I knew a solution, what might it be?*

Keys to Solution-Focused Questions

Here are the keys to solution-focused questions:

- **Focus more attention on the solution than the problem.** This doesn't mean you should ignore understanding the problem. It means that you should spend 80 percent of your energy on the solution and 20 percent on the problem, and not vice versa.
- **Stay out of analysis paralysis.** Keep moving forward, learning and adapting rather than sitting in analysis paralysis.
- **Use questions to get resourceful.** By asking solution-focused questions, you switch your mind into a more resourceful state. Your brain suddenly starts drawing on all your resources internally and around you to solve the problem.

Ability and Motivation

Your ability can dramatically impact your motivation. Even if you enjoy learning, it's easy to get stuck or discouraged. You might get stuck because you don't feel like you're progressing or you don't get feedback that you're learning. This can seriously hold you back. For example, learning how to type can feel like taking a step back. It's taking a step back to take two steps forward, though, and success builds momentum. The challenge is that you have to stay with it to work through your sticking point or to remind yourself that the time you spend now will pay off down the line.

Growth Feels Awkward

When you're learning and growing, there are awkward stages. Remember the first time you tried to ice-skate or ride a bike or drive a car or just about anything? That's what growth feels like. It's easy to lose perspective or even forget that there's a learning stage. Don't let this learning stage become a barrier for your results. When growth doesn't feel awkward, you have to ask if you're pushing yourself enough or if you might have found some natural talent.

Intellectual, Emotional, and Physical

One of my mentors gave me a frame for thinking about learning. You can think of learning in three levels: intellectual, emotional, and physical. In the performance world, this might be thought of as fluency. Here's a summary:

Table 14.4 Intellectual, Emotional, and Physical

Category	Description
Intellectual	At this level, you intellectually "get it." You can regurgitate it or repeat the information, but it's just information. You have no emotional connection to it.
Emotional	At this level, you have an emotional connection to the information. It means something to you and you have a feeling about it. It's when information really sinks in because of personal experience.
Physical	This is when you bake it into your body. Your muscle memory and basal ganglia just know what to do. It's when your body can just reach for the alarm clock without thinking.

This explains why you can study a lot of information, yet not actually master it. You haven't put it into practice. You don't have any experience or emotional connections that help you build expert judgment or develop your intuition. It's also why you might stop short of your potential. For example, when I was younger and learning how to play the saxophone, I didn't want to practice. I figured once I could hit a note that was good enough. I got it intellectually. Why practice when I already proved I could do it? Why? Because I didn't build competency. My body never learned how to "just play it." Without building fluency, I never enjoyed the ability to just play the instrument without working too hard and having to think my way through it each time.

From Unconscious Incompetence
to Unconscious Competence

There's a theory in psychology that explains the four stages of competence:

1. **Unconscious Incompetence.** You don't know what you don't know.
2. **Conscious Incompetence.** You know what you don't know.
3. **Conscious Competence.** You know how to do it, but you have to think your way through it.
4. **Unconscious Competence.** You can do it without thinking. You just know what to do.

One of my favorite examples is learning how to drive. When you first learn how to drive a stick shift, you very quickly learn that you don't know how to do it (conscious incompetence). As you practice you can start to think your way through it (conscious competence). As driving the stick shift becomes a habit, eventually you can drive without thinking, shifting gears effortlessly while you think about other things (unconscious competence).

Flow

The "flow" state is what many of us crave. It's when you're in the zone. The key to finding your flow state is learning something to the point it's baked in. A skill is baked in when you can do it without thinking about it. Flow happens when you're challenged enough to be fully engaged, but not so challenged that you get overwhelmed. The level of challenge you take on combined with your level of integration gives you flow. So the trick is to choose a goal that's appropriate for your level of competence, one where you can get to a flow state before you quit.

Competence vs. Chance

Were you lucky or was it skill? Whichever label you choose to assign to your results can have a big impact on your motivation. Here are some important concepts and theories that I draw from:

Table 14.5 Ways to Look at Competence and Chance

Category	Description
Attribution Theory	Attribution theory is a term in social psychology for how people explain the behaviors of others or of themselves. It's also how they explain why things happen. For our discussion, it's what they attribute their results to.
Attribution Theory of Motivation	Bernard Weiner expands on the attribution theory as it relates to motivation; there are three dimensions for characterizing success or failure: (1) locus; (2) stability; and (3) controllability. Locus is whether it's internal or external (it's the location or position). Stability is whether you view something as changeable over time and how volatile or stable it is. Controllability is whether something is within your control, such as through skills and competence, or outside of your control, such as luck.
Internal vs. External	This is whether you attribute results internally, such as within the person (your disposition), or whether it's external, such as an outside factor (the situation).
Self-Perpetuating	You get what you expect, and it's self-perpetuating. If you don't practice because you don't think it will make a difference, then you won't improve.

Luck Is When Skill and Opportunity Come Together

My favorite definition of luck is what my friend's dad always used to say, "Luck is when skill and opportunity come together." I heard it long ago, but remembered it throughout my life. You won't hit the ball out of the park if you don't get up to bat, and just because you get up to bat doesn't mean you'll hit it out of the park.

Regardless of the theory, find what works for you. If you're dismissing things as luck or situation, when you really can influence the outcome, start stepping up to the plate. If you are beating yourself up over things that you don't control, then stop. Most importantly, what you can own and control is your attitude, your actions, and response. In other words, control your actions and make your best plays. Focus on your approach over results. At the same time, your results are feedback. Use your results as feedback to refine your approach, but don't get overly focused on results.

Metaphors for Motivation

A metaphor is a word or group of words which creates a picture and evokes emotion. For example, a "slippery slope" invokes the image of a hill that is precarious and easy to slide down quickly; so people use it to refer to situations that easily lead down dangerous and irreversible paths. With this emotive use of words, you can use metaphors to represent powerful states. In fact, it is likely that you already use metaphors often in your thoughts and conversations.

Why Metaphors

It's about language and the pictures we hold in our minds. Creating a vision and holding it in our heads will tend to steer us towards the emotions and feelings that we associate with such a picture. Whether or not the picture is an accurate representation of what we are relating it to, we tend to create that picture anyway—and the emotions that go along with it. It therefore has a tendency to become reality, at least on an emotional level. The bottom line is, metaphors shape your overall experience, filter what you perceive, and influence how you make meaning. You are the most important meaning maker (and perhaps not always the best, especially if it's by default and not by design). Choose your metaphors thoughtfully; here's why:

1. They shape your experience.
2. They empower you to change how you think and feel (and your thinking and feeling impact your doing).
3. They help you make meaning.

Example Metaphors

Here are some examples of common metaphors:

Table 14.6 Example Metaphors

Positive Metaphors	Negative metaphors
• Chipping away at the stone • Grab the bull by the horns • Expedition • Mission • Eye of the tiger • Your ship has come in • Your ship is sailing and you're on it	• Uphill battle • Hitting a wall • Swimming upstream • Up the stream without a paddle • Life sucks then you die • You're on your own • That ship has sailed

Whether a metaphor is positive or negative is up to you. For example, most people would probably think of an uphill battle as negative. Then again, some people might like the challenge. Ultimately, it's your context and how you think about a particular metaphor that decides whether it's positive or negative.

How to Use Metaphors Effectively

Here are the keys to using metaphors more effectively:

- **Have a working set of metaphors.** It's important to have a reliable set that you can draw from. If you can't figure out your own, ask your friends for some of theirs.
- **Pick your metaphors carefully.** For better or worse, the metaphors you choose shape your experiences and your reactions.
- **Choose positive metaphors appropriate to the situation.** Pay attention to feedback, your results, and change direction as needed.
- **Choose metaphors that inspire you or hold deep meaning.** Metaphors are strongest when they are tied to your emotions.
- **Get rid of metaphors that aren't working and find new ones.** If you're not getting closer to the feeling states you want, then change the metaphors you're using.

Heroes

Have some heroes. Find the best of the best. Find the people who inspire you and that you can learn from. These can be comic book heroes or real-world ordinary people. Many people go from ordinary to extraordinary by doing great things. In fact, a lot of what makes somebody a hero in somebody's eyes is that they do something great despite the odds or against the odds. Some of our favorite heroes are the ones that triumph over something. Whether your battle is good versus evil or simply trying to change your game, find the people that inspire you to new levels. Use models to help you unleash your best.

Have a Collection of Heroes

Use the most relevant hero for the job at hand. For example, if you have a productivity challenge, find a productivity hero. If you have a relationships challenge, find a relationships hero. It's a buffer of expertise and inspiration. Find the heroes that have the relevant super powers where you need them most.

Everybody Has Flaws

One of the key lessons from one of my mentors is that everybody has flaws. Heroes rise, and heroes fall. You don't have to find "great people." Instead, look for people that do "great things." In other words, don't let flaws get in the way of learning what you can, from anyone you can.

Be YOUR Best

It's not about being as good as or even better than your heroes at something. Instead, it's about unleashing your personal best. And your heroes are your guides to show you your options and to see what's possible; they are not your dictators. There is no reason to stay in their shadow. I say again—it's about being YOUR personal best.

In Summary

- Choose more effective mindsets and metaphors to improve your results in any situation; they are your most important filters shaping your experience.
- Change your mindsets by changing the question or changing your hat.
- Ask more solution-focused questions to control your focus and put yourself into a resourceful state that concentrates on moving forward, adapting, and solving the problem.
- Defeat learned helplessness by adopting a growth mindset and by treating problems as specific, situational, and temporary.
- Remember that growth can feel awkward at times. Be assured, however, that your confidence and motivation does increase as you move through the four stages of competence and find your flow.
- Be careful whether you internalize or externalize your success, and whether you chalk things up to luck. A healthy view on good luck is to view it as skill and opportunity coming together.

Appendix

In This Part:

- **Cheat Sheets**
  Summarizes key information into quick reference sheets.
- **Templates**
  Provides empty templates to help you organize your daily, weekly, monthly, and yearly results.
- **How-Tos**
  Provides step-by-step instructions to help you implement key solutions from the guide.

Cheat Sheet – Agile Results at a Glance

The following is a tickler list of the system, the key concepts, and the practices.

Mental Model

This mental model is a simple way to remember Agile Results:

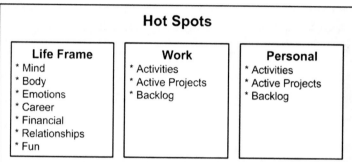

Hot Spots

Life Frame	**Work**	**Personal**
* Mind	* Activities	* Activities
* Body	* Active Projects	* Active Projects
* Emotions	* Backlog	* Backlog
* Career		
* Financial		
* Relationships		
* Fun		

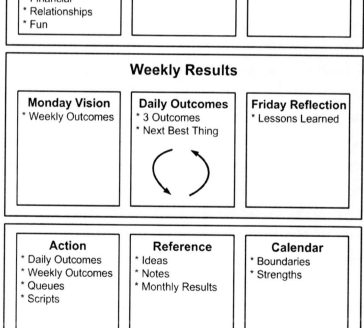

Weekly Results

Monday Vision	**Daily Outcomes**	**Friday Reflection**
* Weekly Outcomes	* 3 Outcomes	* Lessons Learned
	* Next Best Thing	

Action	**Reference**	**Calendar**
* Daily Outcomes	* Ideas	* Boundaries
* Weekly Outcomes	* Notes	* Strengths
* Queues	* Monthly Results	
* Scripts		

Weekly Workflow

Hot Spots	Monday Vision	Daily Outcomes					Friday Reflection	
Personal	3 for the Week	M	T	W	T	F	Going Well / Improve	
Work	1. 2. 3.	1. 2. 3.	1. 2. 3.	1. 2. 3.	1. 2. 3.	1. 2. 3.	1. 2. 3.	1. 2. 3.
Personal								

Plan	Do	Review

Key Concepts

Category	Items
The System	• The Rule of 3 • Hot Spots • Monday Vision, Daily Outcomes, Friday Reflection • Daily Outcomes • Weekly Outcomes • Queues • Action • Reference • Schedule
Key Concepts	• Time as a First-Class Citizen • Fresh Start • Test your results • Fix Time, Flex Scope • Boundaries • Tests for Success • Outcomes Over Activities • Approach Over Results • The Rhythm of Results • Time, Energy, and Technique • Strengths Over Weaknesses • System Over Ad-Hoc • Continuous Learning

Values, Principles, and Practices

Category	Items
10 Values	1. Action Over Analysis Paralysis 2. Approach Over Results 3. Energy Over Time 4. Focus Over Quantity 5. Good Enough Over Perfection 6. Growth Mindset Over Fixed Mindset 7. Outcomes Over Activities 8. Strengths Over Weaknesses 9. System Over Ad-Hoc 10. Value Up Over Backlog Burndown
10 Principles	1. 80/20 Action 2. Change Your Approach 3. Continuous Learning 4. Deliver Incremental Value 5. Factor Action from Reference 6. Set boundaries 7. Fix Time, Flex Scope 8. Less is more 9. Rhythm of Results 10. Version Your Results
12 Practices	1. The Rule of 3 2. Monday Vision, Daily Outcomes, Friday Reflection 3. Scannable Outcomes 4. Daily Outcomes 5. Weekly Outcomes 6. Strong week 7. Timebox Your Day 8. Triage 9. Monthly Improvement Sprints 10. Growth Mindset 11. Action Lists 12. Reference Collections

Supporting Practices

Category	Practices
Rhythm of Results	• Monday Vision, Daily Outcomes, Friday Reflection • Daily, Weekly, Monthly Results
Mind Sets and Motivation	• Compelling "Why" • Switch Hats • Growth Mindset
Time	• Boundaries • Timebox Your Day • Allocated Time • Fix Time, Flex Scope • Buffers
Energy	• Strong Week • Power Hours • Park It
Learning	• 30 Day Improvement Sprints • Improvement Scripts • Lessons Learned • Pair Up
Planning	• The Rule of 3 • Daily Outcomes • Weekly Outcomes • Tests for Success • Diversify Your Results • Reduce Open Work
Doing	• Do It, Review It, Improve It • Just Start • Scripts • Fail Fast • Test Your Results • Batch and Focus • Chunk It Down • Sweeping • Good Enough for Now

Organizing	• Scannable Outcomes
	• One Place to Look
	• Action Lists
	• Reference Lists
Prioritizing	• MUST, SHOULD, COULD
	• Worst Things First
	• Next Best Thing
	• Triage

Cheat Sheet – Supporting Practices Defined

This is in addition to the 12 core practices found in "Chapter 3 – Values, Principles, and Practices of Agile Results."

Supporting Practices for Agile Results Summary Table

Category	Practices
Rhythm of Results	• Daily, Weekly, Monthly Results
Mindsets and Motivation	• Compelling "Why" • Switch Hats
Time	• Allocated Time • Boundaries • Buffers • Fix Time, Flex Scope
Energy	• Park It • Power Hours
Learning	• Improvement Scripts • Lessons Learned • Pair Up
Planning	• Diversify Your Results • Reduce Open Work • Tests for Success
Doing	• Batch and Focus • Chunk It Down • Do It, Review It, Improve It • Fail Fast • Good Enough for Now • Just Start • Scripts • Sweeping • Test Your Results
Organizing	• One Place to Look
Prioritizing	• MUST, SHOULD, COULD • Next Best Thing • Worst Things First

Supporting Practices for Agile Results Defined

The Agile Results practices support each other. You don't need to adopt them all. The following are supporting practices for Agile Results:

1. **Allocated Time.** If it's important, make time for it. If you schedule it, it happens. Block time for key things on your calendar. One practice that works well for a lot of people is to block a few hours in a row for execution. Another practice that works well is to set aside time for a particular type of task and batch it all at once rather than do it throughout the week. One thing that might surprise you is scheduling your free time. You might find you have less free time than you think, and this is a quick reality check to make more free time.

2. **Buffers.** Buffers are the padding you put in your time to allow for surprises. You can buffer with time. For example, you can allow yourself 30 minutes to get to work instead of 10; this way, if there's traffic, you don't get frustrated. You can also create a buffer by keeping your plate only three-quarters full. If you keep your plate completely full, you may not like what spills over; you may also make find yourself lashing out at any threats in terms of more work. Thus, you are unable to respond as effectively to new opportunities. Another way to add buffers is to have transitions. For example, maybe working out after work helps you transition to your personal life. The simple act of adding buffers can help reduce friction, stress, and anxiety in your life.

3. **Boundaries.** This means setting minimums and maximums on how you spend your time. Setting boundaries helps keep a sustainable pace. It also ensures that you spend time in some areas that you might otherwise ignore or forget about. By spending enough time and energy in the right categories, you get synergy. For example, by spending time in your relationships, things get easier at work. By spending time on your body, you keep your mind fresh. By spending enough time in fun, you keep your energy strong.

4. **Batch and Focus.** Consolidate similar tasks. This helps you focus rather than task switch. It also helps you find efficiencies. When you do something more, you find ways to improve.

5. **Chunk It Down.** Chunk your work down. You build momentum as you get results. You can chunk your work down in terms of complexity, such as creating incremental hurdles. You can also

chunk down time, such as setting mini-milestones. Another approach is to simply quantify it: for example, three actions, three outcomes, etc.

6. **Compelling "Why."** Find a "Why" that drives you. This can be as simple as deciding that you want to master your craft. The key is to internalize it, rather than focus on external rewards. This will help see you through the dark times as well as help you live your values.

7. **Daily, Weekly, Monthly Results.** Establish a rhythm of results. Each day, week, and month is a new chance for results. If you fall off the horse, you can get back on. If you miss a train, catch the next one. Having a rhythm for your results helps you build routines and improve your ability to get results. I think of the rhythm of results in terms of daily, weekly, and monthly results. Using The Rule of 3, I can try to accomplish three meaningful results each day, each week, and each month. It adds up fast. Most importantly, it's a very simple way to frame out results. Rather than get caught up in the details, it's easy to step back and think in terms of three items. Then, whether I'm looking at a day, a week or a month, I can quickly look at the bigger picture. For example, the three results for the month are much higher level than the three outcomes for the week, which are much higher than the three outcomes for each day. It's a quick way to traverse a bunch of action that's spread over time, and not get bogged down in the tasks themselves. It's a sketch of your results that you can incrementally render daily, weekly, and monthly.

8. **Diversify Your Results.** This is the key to balance. If you look at your results across your life as a portfolio, you can choose where to invest more and where to cut back. You can use different lenses. For life in general, I check how I'm investing in mind, body, emotions, career, financial, relationships, and fun. At work, I check how I'm spending energy across administration, relationships, thinking and doing. In terms of projects, I try to have a vital few that I spend most of my focus on, as well as a few innovation projects for learning and growing. I try not to have all my eggs in a single basket. This means I'm not overly invested in one thing, and I can keep perspective and balance while remaining responsive to change.

9. **Do It, Review It, Improve It.** Decide and go. When you perform tasks, take the action, and then analyze your results.

Don't critique yourself throughout the process. Perform, then evaluate.

10. **Fail Fast.** Fail early and fail often. Failure is part of the learning process. The sooner you hit your glass ceilings or tackle your high risks, the sooner you can adjust as needed. Learn and move on.

11. **Good Enough for Now.** One way to deal with perfectionism is to focus on good enough for now. You can improve it later, once you get some feedback; just get something to done first. Remember, what might be right for you might not be right for some; perfection is in the eye of the beholder.

12. **Just Start.** Taking action is the key. Just get started. This will help you avoid analysis paralysis. You can always correct course once you get going.

13. **Improvement Scripts.** Write down steps to perform a specific action or routine.

14. **Lessons Learned.** Identify three things that worked well. Identify three things that didn't work well. Carry forward your lessons learned.

15. **Monthly Results.** Each month, review your results. One simple way is to create a tickler list that shows your most important results for the month. This helps you keep score. This also helps you see the forest from the trees. Each month is a good time to take stock of your accomplishments and reflect on what if anything you need to change going forward.

16. **MUST, SHOULD, COULD.** Use MUST, SHOULD, and COULD to prioritize your potential tasks; use it with your to-do list if you have one. Then, focus on your three MUSTs for the day. I've found it much more helpful to think in terms of MUST, SHOULD, and COULD; however, if you need to use a prioritization system that is number centric (for example, priority 1, priority 2, and priority 3; or p1, p2, p3), then you can still think in terms of MUST, SHOULD, and COULD by mapping it accordingly. If you get really good at focusing on your MUSTs, you'll see immediate improvement. Where people fall down is they mix too many SHOULDs and COULDs into their work each day without realizing it, so they don't actually ever get any meaningful work done. If you are having trouble, The Rule of 3 helps. Getting three MUSTs done each day quickly builds momentum. It's a sense of accomplishment. You may find as you get more effective, you start to bite off more. Note: If the word MUST creates a sense of

heaviness for you or you find you no longer look forward to getting your results, then change your language. For example, rather than your MUST dos, think of your CHOOSE TOs. This puts you back in power, and this simple reframing can help you get your energy back.

17. **Next Best Thing.** Remind yourself to value your time. Ask yourself, "What's the next best thing to do?" It's a cutting question that helps you prioritize in the moment.

18. **One Place to Look.** Whether you have a paper system or an electronic system, the key is to have one place to look for all your action items and your reference information. This works in conjunction with keeping your information scannable.

19. **Pair Up.** Pairing up or teaming up can be a great way to complement your strengths and get results. The key is to pair up with the right people. This is especially effective for learning new things; in this case, you find a mentor. This also works well on projects; if you're a starter, look for a finisher (or vice versa).

20. **Park It.** Sometimes it makes sense to park something you're working on, at least for the time being. You can come back to it later. If it feels like you're churning and not making progress, it might make sense just to park it for now.

21. **Power Hours.** Focus on increasing your power hours. A power hour is where you feel like you're incredibly productive and you're in the zone. You might find that you have certain power hours throughout the day. Maybe you have power hours in the morning, or maybe you are better in the afternoon or at night. The first step is just noticing when they occur. Some power hours might be due to the type of activity you work on, while others might be driven by your biorhythms. Either way, once you know the pattern for your power hours, you can find ways to optimize to have more power hours. By adding more power hours, you can spend less overall time on your tasks. This improves your efficiency and your effectiveness.

22. **Reduce Open Work.** Reduce the work you have in flight. It's better to finish one thing before spinning up a bunch of other things. The more work you have that's not finished, the more chances you won't finish. When you reduce work that's in flight, you can better focus on the task at hand and bring it to completion. Task switching is an enemy of results.

23. **Scripts.** You can write your routines down as a set of steps. Writing routines down can help find ways to improve. You can also avoid thrashing or spending too much think time while you're trying to perform the routine. You can also use your scripts to avoid common mistakes.

24. **Sweeping.** Things get messy. Sweeping is a way to periodically clean things up. For example, you might sweep your lists once a week. You might sweep your notes once a month. You might spend a night every other week cleaning up open issues on your project. Sweeping is a tremendously powerful technique because it frees you up from over-engineering perfection up front or trying to over-police something with a bunch of gates. You let the work run its course; then you do a cleanup when you have a better vantage point or when you can batch the work. This also helps you avoid death by a thousand paper cuts.

25. **Switch Hats.** One technique to change your mindset is to imagine putting on an imaginary hat. Maybe in school you remember putting your thinking cap on. You can use different hats for different purposes. For example, you might need an analytical hat. You might also need a hat for "kicking arse and taking names." You might need a hat for more tedious or mundane activities. Switching hats will help you switch modes. You'll improve your overall effectiveness by changing your mindset to match the challenge in front of you. Note that some people like to literally wear different hats for different purposes.

26. **Test Your Results.** Test your results quickly to find out what you know, don't know, and need to know next. It's easy to talk yourself out of something or to analyze yourself into a string of impossibilities. Instead, do a quick dry run, or try a show and tell of your results to see what you can do. One effective way is to timebox and see what sort of results you can produce in an hour. This will quickly tell you where your bottlenecks might be or where you need help.

27. **Tests for Success.** If you know what good looks like, it's easier to move towards your target. A lot of failed results are actually failures to define success. You can think of this as test-driven results. Basically, you should have a strawman in mind of what good looks like; then, you readjust as you go along and learn more.

28. **Worst Things First.** Start your day with the worst things first. It's when you have the most energy. Rather than having something loom over you throughout the day, you can take it off your plate early and enjoy the rest of your day.

Template – Daily Planner

Identify three outcomes for the day. List all the tasks and activities that you need to perform. Use your three outcomes to focus and prioritize your tasks and activities.

Day	Outcomes
Outcomes	1. 2. 3.
Tasks	• • • • • • • • • •

Template – Weekly Planner

Your weekly planner will help you identify results and actions for each day. The most important step is to simply identify three results you want for the week. You can then identify three results you want for each day. By identifying the three results you want each day, you can choose more effective actions or tasks. Simply fill out as much or as little as you know.

Monday Vision

Identify three results for the week:
1. Outcome 1 –
2. Outcome 2 –
3. Outcome 3 –

Week at a Glance

Each day, identify three outcomes for that day.

Day	Outcomes
Monday	1. 2. 3.
Tuesday	1. 2. 3.
Wednesday	1. 2. 3.
Thursday	1. 2. 3.
Friday	1. 2. 3.

Friday Reflection

Identify three things going well:

1.
2.
3.

Identify three things to improve:

1.
2.
3.

Template – Monthly Planner

You can model your results for the month by focusing on three results for the month and then three results for each week. When you're just starting out, you might find it easier to simply list the three results you want for the month. Gradually, you can start to see how your results each week feed into the results you want for the month.

A simple way to work through the monthly planner is to list things you would like done for the month in your Queue. Prioritize the items by MUST, SHOULD, or COULD. Limit your MUST to the three most important outcomes. Under "Planned," decide three outcomes you want for each week of the month. Under "Completed," list your actual results at the end of each week, against your outcomes. This will help you reflect on whether you are getting the right results or if you need to adjust your targets or your approach.

Outcomes

Identify three outcomes for the month:
1. Outcome 1 –
2. Outcome 2 –
3. Outcome 3 –

Month at a Glance

Queue	Week	Planned	Completed
MUST • •	Week 1	• • •	• • •
• SHOULD	Week 2	• • •	• • •
• • •	Week 3	• • •	• • •
COULD • • •	Week 4	• • •	• • •

Template – Yearly Planner

The goal is to create a scannable year at a glance, where you can see the key activities and events for your year. This will help you better anticipate and plan. The most important step it to identify three outcomes for the year. A simple way to do this is ask yourself, if the year were over, what are three results you want under your belt?

To complete the template, first, list your personal events that you can think of. This can include recurring items, such as bills or taxes or birthdays. Next, list any work activities and events that you can think of. You can think of this as a map of results for your year. You can simply list any key outcomes that you want for certain months. Think of it as a rough sketch unless you have hard dates set for things. This helps you visualize your time for the year.

Outcomes

Identify three outcomes for the year:
1. Outcome 1 –
2. Outcome 2 –
3. Outcome 3 –

Year at a Glance

When	Outcomes	Work Events	Personal Events
January	1. 2. 3.	• • •	• • •
February	1. 2. 3.	• • •	• • •
March	1. 2. 3.	• • •	• • •

April	1. 2. 3.	• • •	• • •
May	1. 2. 3.	• • •	• • •
June	1. 2. 3.	• • •	• • •
July	1. 2. 3.	• • •	• • •
August	1. 2. 3.	• • •	• • •
September	1. 2. 3.	• • •	• • •
October	1. 2. 3.	• • •	• • •
November	1. 2. 3.	• • •	• • •
December	1. 2. 3.	• • •	• • •

Template – Schedule at a Glance

You can use the Schedule at a Glance template as a guide to baseline your weekly schedule and help you identify where your time goes. Whether you use paper, a whiteboard, or an electronic form, identify the regularly recurring things in your life (such as events and appointments); identify your true free time as well. It's like looking at your portfolio; you can see where you invest your time. Once you can see your weekly schedule at a glance, you can then make more thoughtful decisions about where you spend more or less of your time—designing a more effective week that supports you.

	Sun	Mon	Tue	Wed	Thu	Fri	Sat
7:00 a.m.							
8:00							
9:00							
10:00							
11:00							
12:00							
1:00 p.m.							
2:00							
3:00							
4:00							
5:00							
6:00							
7:00							
8:00							
9:00							
10:00							

How To – Adopt Agile Results

Summary

This article shows you how to adopt the Agile Results system. Agile Results is a simple results system. You can adopt the basics of Agile Results in under five minutes. You can adopt or tailor pieces as you see fit. By adopting The Rule of 3; the Monday Vision, Daily Outcomes, Friday Reflection pattern; and the life Hot Spots, you establish a rhythm of results and achieve work life balance. Agile Results is action-oriented with an emphasis on outcomes over activities, while supporting continuous growth and learning. Agile Results also helps you manage your energy across your work and life, giving you the power to achieve whatever you want with sustainable results.

Contents

- Objectives
- Summary of Steps
- Step 1—Adopt The Rule of 3
- Step 2—Adopt the Monday Vision, Daily Outcomes, Friday Reflection Pattern
- Step 3—Adopt the Life Hot Spots

Objectives

- Learn how to adopt The Rule of 3 to focus and prioritize your action.
- Learn how to adopt the Monday Vision, Daily Outcomes, Friday Reflection pattern to establish a rhythm of results.
- Learn how to adopt life Hot Spots to achieve work-life balance and spend your time and energy on the most important things in your life.

Overview

Agile Results is a simple and effective results system for personal productivity. It works by establishing a rhythm of results, prioritizing value, and taking simple, consistent actions towards your results. By treating time as a first-class citizen, you can set effective boundaries and achieve work-life balance. By having a system you can count on, it helps you get back on your feet again. The simplicity is part of its effectiveness. The heart of the system is the synergy of three things: The Rule of 3; the Monday Vision, Daily Outcomes, Friday Reflection pattern; and life Hot Spots.

The Rule of 3 is about identifying three outcomes each day. By starting your day with three outcomes, you clarify what you want to accomplish. When you know what you want to accomplish, you can prioritize more effectively, and you can let things go. Rather than focus on your endless backlog or overload, you shift your focus to the three most valuable things you can do today. Each day is a fresh start; so is each week, each month, and each year. It's your chance to wipe the slate clean and cherry-pick your most important items. Rather than focus on everything that you haven't finished, you focus on answering the question, "What's the next best thing for you to do?" The most important thing about The Rule of 3 is that you are focusing on outcomes over activities. You are also limiting what's on your focus so that you don't overwhelm yourself. When you finish your three outcomes, you can always grab more. This is about setting your sights on three meaningful results for you, and using that to drive your day. It can be as simple as (1) have a great lunch experience with a friend; (2) complete 10 draft pages for your next book; and (3) complete an outline of your project plan.

The Monday Vision, Daily Outcomes, Friday Reflection pattern is a simple weekly results system. On Mondays, you identify the three most important results for the week. Each day, you identify the three most important outcomes for the day. On Fridays, you reflect by asking yourself what are three things going well and what are three things to improve?

Life Hot Spots is a heat map for your life and a way to invest your time and energy in areas that matter: mind, body, emotions, career, financial, relationships, and fun. When you invest in these areas, the sum is more than the parts. By spending time in fun, you keep your mind and emotions in good shape. By investing in your mind, body, and relationships, you perform better at work. The most important concept for the life Hot Spots is to set boundaries in terms of time or energy. For example, you might need to set a boundary on how much time you spend at work, using a rule such as "Dinner on the table at 5:30." You might want to set a minimum of time in your relationships, such as "Tuesday night is date night."

Summary of Steps

- Step 1—Adopt The Rule of 3
- Step 2—Adopt the Monday Vision, Daily Outcomes, Friday Reflection pattern
- Step 3—Adopt life Hot Spots

Step 1—Adopt The Rule of 3

The simplest way to adopt Agile Results is to start using The Rule of 3 to start your day. The Rule of 3 is about identifying three outcomes each day. Each day is a fresh start, and three is an effective limit. The Rule of 3 has been used with success in a variety of contexts. It's sticky, and people tend to be good at remembering things in threes. To use The Rule of 3, start your day by asking either, "What are three outcomes I want for the day?" or, "What are three results I want for the day?" While it's recommended that you write them down, it's more important that you internalize them, so you don't have to look them up. A simple check is if you can say your three outcomes for the day, whether you're in the hall or in your car or wherever you are.

Apply The Rule of 3 to the Day, the Week, the Month, and the Year

You can use The Rule of 3 to help you see the forest from the trees. By identifying your top three results you want for the day, the week, the month, and the year, you keep better perspective.

When	Examples
Day	• • •
Week	• • •
Month	• • •
Year	• • • Examples: learn to fly, mentor someone at work, spend one week with an old friend
	Only write down three! Also, remember the life Hot Spots: mind, body, emotions, career, financial, relationships, and fun.

Don't overwhelm yourself. The Rule of 3 is about identifying only and no more than three outcomes each day.

Guidelines

Here are some guidelines for adopting The Rule of 3:

• They are your tests for success.
• You can prioritize any incoming actions against your desired results.
• When you get distracted throughout the day, you can remind yourself what you wanted to accomplish.
• If you already have tasks lists, you can simply add your three outcomes to the top. This reminds you what you're driving for.

- You learn your focus and capacity. If you aren't completing the three results you set for the day, you might be picking the wrong things, or you might be biting off more than you can chew.

If you're not sure where to start, pick one thing for yourself, one thing for your family, and one thing for your job each day.

Checkpoint

- *Can you say your three outcomes for today out loud?*
- *Are your three outcomes the three most important things you really want to accomplish today?*
- *Are your three outcomes actually results or achievements (not activities or tasks)?*

Step 2—Adopt the Monday Vision, Daily Outcomes, Friday Reflection Pattern

This is your pattern for weekly results. The idea is that each week is a fresh start. To adopt the Monday Vision, Daily Outcomes, Friday Reflection pattern, at the start of the week, identify your three most important outcomes for the week. In other words, if you look ahead to Friday, what three results would you like to have achieved? At the start of each day, identify your three most important results. On Fridays, start your day by asking yourself, "What are three things going well?" and, "What are three things to improve?" You can then feed your results into the next week. For example, if you find that you are accomplishing your three results for the week, are they the right things? Can you push back on what's on your plate? If, instead, you find that you aren't finishing your three results each day, is it because you are getting distracted? Are you not picking the right three things to begin with? This is your continuous improvement loop. The more effective feedback you provide yourself, the more you can improve your results. Each week is a new chance to tune your results and learn more about your capacity and bottlenecks.

Summary of the Monday Vision,
Daily Outcomes, Friday Reflection

The following table summarizes the Monday Vision, Daily Outcomes, Friday Reflection pattern:

Item	Actions
Monday Vision	Identify 3 compelling outcomes or results for the week.
Daily Outcomes	Identify 3 compelling outcomes each day.
Friday Reflection	Identify 3 things going well and 3 things to improve.

Guidelines

- Stick with three outcomes for the week. Don't create a laundry list of results. Identify the three most meaningful outcomes. You can always bite off more, after you complete your three results.
- Identify your three outcomes for the day, at the very start of your day, before you are overwhelmed or in the thick of things. This is how you drive your day versus react to it.
- When you identify three things going well, try to find the success pattern so that you are conscious of why and how.
- When you identify three things to improve, try to find the specific patterns that aren't working so that you can identify specific actions to change, whether it's thinking, feeling or doing.

Checkpoint

- *Do you know your three most important outcomes for the week?*
- *Do you know your three most important outcomes each day?*
- *Do you know your three key things going well?*
- *Do you know your three key things to improve?*

Step 3—Adopt Life Hot Spots

Life Hot Spots are a set of high priority categories that help determine where to spend your time and energy. By setting effective boundaries, you'll achieve work-life balance and improve your results in all areas of your life. The life Hot Spots are

- Mind
- Body
- Emotions
- Career
- Financial
- Relationships
- Fun

By investing in these areas, you set yourself up for success, and you help limit the impact of potential downturns. This also gives you a concrete way to achieve work-life balance, in the worst of times and in the best of times. To adopt the life Hot Spots, simply use the categories as a lens to identify your pain or opportunities, what actions or outcomes you want to focus on, and set more effective boundaries.

Setting Boundaries

You should set minimums and maximums for your Hot Spots in terms of time and energy. This keeps you from getting over-invested. Use your Hot Spots to set boundaries. Set a maximum on career and a minimum on relationships, body, and fun. In the right categories, setting a minimum helps you to avoid getting unbalanced and to improve other categories, while setting a maximum encourages you to learn to be more effective. For example, if you only have eight hours to throw at your day, you'll use them wisely. The worst mistake is to throw more time at problems. The key is to reduce time spent, while increasing value and improving your efficiency and effectiveness.

Hot Spots	Boundaries (per week)
Mind	
Body	Minimum of 3 hours
Emotions	
Career	Maximum of 50 hours
Financial	
Relationships	Minimum of 8 hours
Fun	Minimum of 3 hours

In this case, step one is deciding to spend no more than 50 hours each week on your career Hot Spot. Now it forces you to bite off only what you can chew. This is how you start improving plate management and pushing back effectively. You can only spread your life force over so much. The categories help support each other. If not properly allocated, they can also work against each other.

Guidelines
- Set a maximum of time to spend on career.
- Set a minimum of time to spend on your relationships.
- Set a minimum of time to spend on fun.
- Set a minimum of time to spend on your body.
- Test your results. If the time limits you set aren't working, adjust them and test again.

Checkpoint
- *Are you investing the right amount of time in the right places?*
- *Are you reducing your worst pain points?*
- *Are you leveraging your best opportunities?*
- *Does your investment of time and energy actually reflect what you want to accomplish?*

How To – Adopt the 12 Core Practices of Agile Results

Summary

This article shows you how to adopt the 12 core practices of Agile Results: you'll review the 12 core practices, and then systematically adopt the practices. You don't have to adopt the practices all at once, but the more you adopt, the better the results. These practices are complementary. By putting the practices in place, you structure yourself for success. When you fall off the horse, you have a system in place that will help you get back on.

Contents

- Objectives
- Overview
- Summary of Steps
- Step 1—Review the 12 Core Practices
- Step 2—Create Your List of Scannable Outcomes
- Step 3—Adopt Daily Outcomes
- Step 4—Adopt Weekly Outcomes
- Step 5—Design Your Week
- Organizing Your Action and Reference Information
- Adopting 30 Day Improvement Sprints
- Adopting Additional Practices

Objectives

- Learn how to adopt the 12 core practices of Agile Results.
- Learn how to have a more effective day.
- Learn how to have a more effective week.
- Learn how to spend more time in things that matter most to you.
- Learn how to reduce open work and executing the work you have way more effectively.

Overview

The 12 core practices of Agile Results are

1. Action Lists
2. Daily Outcomes
3. Growth Mindset
4. Monday Vision, Daily Outcomes, Friday Reflection
5. Monthly Improvement Sprint
6. Reference Collections
7. Scannable Outcomes
8. Strong Week
9. The Rule of 3
10. Timebox Your Day
11. Triage
12. Weekly Outcomes

The core practices of Agile Results help you build a personal results system for daily, weekly, monthly, and yearly results. It combines practices from software engineering, sports psychology, and positive psychology, as well as principles, patterns, and practices for time management and personal productivity. It's holistic in that it combines time, energy, and techniques to produce more effective results at work and home. By investing in your life Hot Spots (mind, body, emotions, career, financial, relationships and fun), you end up with a system for sustainable results. In addition, you consistently renew your skills and energy as you spend more time in your strengths and the things you enjoy, while learning and responding to changing environments.

Stop taking on more until you finish what's on your plate: eat the hot stuff first and let stuff slough off. Letting the right things go is realistic, practical, and effective; people that don't let stuff go, tend to be the ones that fail—everything ends up a priority so there is no priority. Get more effective at cycling through what's on your plate, so you can flow results. It's this little idea of reducing open work and executing the work you have way more effectively. Some ways to do this include the following: reduce task switching; play to your strengths (as this renews your energy, and you get these things done faster than other people can); say "No" effectively (by pushing for your strengths and setting/getting clear on your requirements for success: "I can do this, if ..."); and know your capacity (by cycling through The Rule of 3 each day, each week, each month, each year).

Summary of Steps

- Step 1—Review the 12 Core Practices
- Step 2—Create Your List of Scannable Outcomes
- Step 3—Adopt Daily Outcomes
- Step 4—Adopt Weekly Outcomes
- Step 5—Design Your Week

Step 1—Review the 12 Core Practices

Familiarize yourself with the 12 core practices of Agile Results. These definitions are found in "Chapter 3 – Values, Principles, and Practices of Agile Results," but I've included it here for convenience:

1. **30 Day Improvement Sprints.** Pick one thing to improve for the month. Each month, pick something new. This gives you a chance to cycle through 12 things over the year. You can always repeat a sprint. The idea is that 30 days is enough time to experiment with your results throughout the month. You might not see progress after the first couple weeks while you're learning. A month is a good chunk of time to check your progress.

2. **Action Lists.** Track your actions with tickler lists. Consider the following action lists: Daily Outcomes, Weekly Outcomes, Queues, and Scripts.

3. **Daily Outcomes.** Each day is a new chance for results. Use daily tickler lists for action items, and create a new list each day. Each day, ask yourself what are three things (The Rule of 3) you want to accomplish? Always start your list with your three most important outcomes for the day. The key to an effective Daily Outcomes list is that you keep your three outcomes for the day at the top, while listing the rest of your to-dos below that. This way you have a reminder of what you want to accomplish.

4. **Growth Mindset.** This is simply a decision. You decide that you'll learn and grow. If you get knocked down, you'll get up again. You decide that no problem is personal, pervasive or permanent. Life's not static. Neither are your results.

5. **Monday Vision, Daily Outcomes, Friday Reflection.** Decide what you want to accomplish for the week. Make progress each day. At the end of the week, reflect on your results.

6. **Reference Lists.** Some information is not actionable. This is reference information. It might be helpful information, and good

to know, but if it's not actionable, then it's reference. You can store your reference information as tickler lists. Here are some example reference lists you might keep: Ideas, Notes, Weekly Results, Monthly Results, and Yearly Results.

7. **Scannable Outcomes.** Think of this as what's on your radar. At a glance, you should be able to see what you want to accomplish and what you're spending your time and energy on. Outcomes guide your action. Keep your outcomes scannable at a glance. Organize outcomes by your work, personal, and life Hot Spots. For example, create a list of outcomes for your life frame (body, career, emotions, financial, fun, mind, and relationships).

8. **Strong Week.** Each week focus on spending more time on activities that make you strong and less time on activities that make you weak. Do the same with people. Spend more time with people that make you strong and less time with people that make you weak. Push activities that make you weak to the first part of your day. By doing your worst things first, you create a glide-path for the rest of the day. Better yet, you don't have activities that weaken you loom over you throughout the day. More importantly, by following activities that make you weak, with activities that make you strong, you can rebuild your energy and spread your energy throughout the day. During your Friday Reflections, you should evaluate your energy levels. Assuming that your regimen for eating, sleeping, and working out aren't getting in the way, are your activities during the week strengthening you or weakening you? You can do a few things. You can try shuffling around when you do certain activities. For example, you might move them to the morning or move them later in the day. You might try pairing up on some activities. You also might find that some activities really are a drain on you and you should limit them. Worst case, consolidate activities that drain you to your mornings so that you can get them over with when you are strongest. Follow them up with activities that strengthen you so you get your strength back.

9. **The Rule of 3.** This Rule of 3 will help you stay focused on the vital few things that matter. Identify your three key outcomes. This is the heart of your Daily Outcomes. Identify three key outcomes each day, each week, each month, and each year. This helps you see the forest from the trees. The three outcomes for the year are bigger than the three outcomes for the month are bigger

than the three outcomes for the week, are bigger than the three outcomes for your day. This also helps you manage scope. It's all too easy to bite off more than you can chew. If you nail the three items you wanted to accomplish, then go ahead and bite off more. Think of it as a buffet of results and you can keep going back, just don't overflow your plate on each trip.

10. **Timebox Your Day.** If you keep time a constant (by ending your day at a certain time), it helps with a lot of things: work-life balance (days can chew into nights can chew into weekends), figuring out where to optimize your day, prioritizing (time is a great forcing function) Carve up your day into big buckets (e.g., administration, work time, think time, connect time), and then figure out how much time you're willing to give them. If you're not getting the throughput you want, you can ask yourself: Are you working on the right things? Are you spending too much time on lesser things? Are there some things you can do more efficiently or effectively? Without a timebox, you can easily spend all day reading mails, blogs, aliases, doing self-training, etc., and then wonder where your day went. Using timeboxes helps strike balance. Timeboxes also help with pacing. If you only have so many hours to produce results, you're more careful to spend my high energy hours on the right things.

11. **Triage.** Triage incoming action items: Do It, Queue It, Schedule It, or Delegate It. Do It, if it's the next best thing for you to do, or now is the most opportunistic time, or if it will cost you more pain, time or effort to do it later. Queue It (add it to your queue), if it's something you need to get done, but now is not the right time. Schedule It, if you need a block of time to get the work done. Delegate It, if it's something that should be done by somebody else.

12. **Weekly Outcomes.** Create a new list each week. Each week is a new chance for results. Always start with your three most important outcomes for the week (The Rule of 3).

Step 2—Create Your List of Scannable Outcomes

In this step, you implement the following practices: Reference Lists, Scannable Outcomes, and The Rule of 3. The key is to identify the outcomes that you want for your life Hot Spots, work Hot Spots and personal Hot Spots. Hot Spots are simply areas of focus, projects, or activities that you need to spend your time and energy on.

Identify Outcomes for Life Hot Spots

For each Hot Spot, identify up to three outcomes (results) you want:

Hot Spot	Outcomes
Mind	
Body	
Emotions	
Career	
Financial	
Relationships	
Fun	

Identify Outcomes for Work Hot Spots

For each project or major activity at work, identify up to three outcomes you want:

Hot Spots	Outcomes
Project/Activity #1	
Project/Activity #2	
Project/Activity #3	

Identify Outcomes for Personal Hot Spots

For each project or major activity at home, identify up to three outcomes you want:

Hot Spots	Outcomes
Project/Activity #1	
Project/Activity #2	
Project/Activity #3	

Step 3—Adopt Daily Outcomes

In this step, you implement the following practices: Daily Outcomes, The Rule of 3, Timebox Your Day, Triage, and Action Lists.

Create a List of Daily Outcomes

Each day, identify and write down your three results you want for the day. If you already have a to-do list system, simply add your three outcomes to the top. This serves as an Action List to remind you of the three key things you want to accomplish for the day. Here is an example:

Date	2009-09-12
Outcomes	1. First draft of chapter, 30% complete. 2. Great lunch with an old friend. 3. Training material reviewed and signed off.
Actions	• Write initial bullet points. • Research the training requirements. • Find the contacts for sign off. • Etc.

Keep the following points in mind:

• Each day, create a new list and name it the current date. This keeps it simple and lets you review your week by each day.

- Each day, identify the three most important results.
- Don't carry over everything each day. Let things slough off based on priority.

Each day you will create a new list of outcomes for the day. The three outcomes help you focus and prioritize everything you do. Make a fresh list each day. Let things slough off. You can carry over an outcome the next day, only if it's one of the three next best things for you to do. The big thing to keep in mind here is that these three outcomes are your tests for success for the day. You get to define what your best results for the day are. You might decide your most important outcome is that you accomplish nothing. It's up to you how you set your bar, but the idea is to be mindful and exercise your choices thoughtfully.

Timebox Your Day

Treat your time as a limited budget. Spend it on the things that are most important to what you want to accomplish. To do so, set limits, either in terms of minimums or maximums. Carve up your day into big buckets (e.g., administration, work time, think time, and connect time); then, figure out how much time you're willing to give them. Here is an example:

Bucket	Time Budget
Overall Workday	8 hours maximum
Administration	1 hour maximum
Planning	30 minutes minimum
Execution	4 hours minimum
Meeting	1 hour maximum

Keep the following points in mind:

- Set an overall limit for your work day. This is your time budget. This will help you prioritize where you spend your time during the day.

- Treat it as a baseline and stay flexible. For example, some days you may need to spend more time in planning. The idea is to know where your time goes.
- Change the amount of time you spend on things. This is one of the simplest and most effective ways to change your results.

Triage Your Incoming Actions

You most likely have to manage incoming action items throughout your day. Triage incoming items against what you want to accomplish for the day.

Technique	Description
Do It	It's the next best thing for you to do, or now is the most opportunistic time, or it will cost you more pain, time or effort to do it later.
Queue It	Add it to your queue if it's something you need to get done, but now is not the right time.
Schedule It	If you need a block of time to get the work done.
Delegate It	If it's something that should be done by somebody else.

Step 4—Adopt Weekly Outcomes

In this step, you implement the following practices: Weekly Outcomes; Monday Vision, Daily Outcomes, Friday Reflection; Growth Mindset; The Rule of 3; and Reference Lists.

Create a List of Weekly Outcomes

Each week, identify and write down your three results you want for the week. This serves as an Action List to remind you what's important for the week.

Date	2009-09-14
Outcomes	1. Training courseware complete. 2. Lawn and garden in top shape. 3. 5 power hours added to my week.

Adopt Monday Vision, Daily Outcomes, Friday Reflection

Use the Monday Vision, Daily Outcomes, Friday Reflection pattern to drive your weekly results. On Mondays, identify the three most important results you want for the week. Each day, identify the three most important results you want for the day. On Fridays, reflect on your results and identify what's going well and what needs to improve. Use what you learned from your Friday Reflection to improve the next week. It's a cycle of improvement. This is how you employ your Growth Mindset for continuous learning.

Item	Description
Monday Vision	• On Monday, identify three outcomes for the week. • Visualize: if this were Friday, what would you like to look back on?
Daily Outcomes	• Each day, identify three outcomes for the day. • Prioritize everything you do against the three outcomes.
Friday Reflection	• On Friday, identify three things going well and three things to improve. • Reflect on your actual results against the results you wanted.

Step 5—Design Your Week

In this step, you implement the following practices: Strong Week and Growth Mindset.

Fix Time for Eating, Sleeping, and Working Out

One of the most effective patterns for improving your week is having consistent times for eating, sleeping, and working out. If you set those in place and work everything else around that, you have a great start. This is how many of the most effective people structure their week. They know how much sleep they need, so this helps them figure out what time to go to bed the night before. By making time for your work out and eating, you're helping ensure that you invest in yourself. One of the most common patterns for successful people is they workout first thing in the morning. This gives them a continuous block of "me" time from the night before into the start of their day.

Set Boundaries and Limits

Set boundaries and limits in terms of time for any life Hot Spots that need attention. Here is an example:

Hot Spot	Minimums and Maximums (per week)
Mind	
Body	Minimum of 3 hours
Emotions	
Career	Maximum of 50 hours
Financial	
Relationships	Minimum of 3 hours
Fun	Minimum of 3 hours

Keep the following points in mind:

• When you set a minimum in the right categories, you avoid getting unbalanced and improving other categories.
• When you set a maximum in the right categories, you learn how to become more effective. For example, if you only have eight hours to throw at your day, you learn to use them wisely.
• The worst mistake it to throw more time at problems. The key is to reduce time spent, while increasing value and improving efficiency and effectiveness.

Design a Strong Week

Map out your strengths and weaknesses. Consolidate your weaknesses. Add strengths.

Day	Schedule
Sunday	
Monday	9:00 – 10:00 a.m.—Worst thing first (weaknesses) 10:00 – 11:00 a.m.—Power hour. 2:00 – 3:00 p.m.—Power hour.
Tuesday	9:00 – 10:00 a.m.—Worst thing first (weaknesses) 10:00 – 11:00 a.m.—Power hour. 2:00 – 3:00 p.m.—Power hour.
Wednesday	9:00 – 10:00 a.m.—Worst thing first (weaknesses) 10:00 – 11:00 a.m.—Power hour. 2:00 – 3:00 p.m.—Power hour.
Thursday	9:00 – 10:00 a.m.—Worst thing first (weaknesses) 10:00 – 11:00 a.m.—Power hour. 2:00 – 3:00 p.m.—Power hour.
Friday	9:00 – 10:00 a.m.—Worst thing first (weaknesses) 10:00 – 11:00 a.m.—Power hour. 2:00 – 3:00 p.m.—Power hour.
Saturday	

Keep the following points in mind:
- A weakness is anything that drains you.
- A strength is an activity that catalyzes you and you're naturally good at. It's your talent. Add strengths to improve your energy and results.
- Get rid of as many activities that are weaknesses as you can. Consolidate the weaknesses you can't get rid of, to the early part of your day, to get them over with.

Organizing Your Action and Reference Information

Reference information is information that's useful to know, but isn't an action item. Action information is anything that represents something you do. If you can't do it, it's not an action. The key is to factor reference from action. In doing so, you can quickly scan for actions you need to take, as well as easily scan for information you need as input. When it comes to results, the keys to effective information management include creating scannable lists (think of these as tickler lists where you just need a quick note to remind you what to do); factoring reference from action; consolidating where to look (i.e., one place to look versus anywhere and everywhere); and periodically sweeping your collections (going back and cleaning things up when they get out of control).

Action Lists	Reference Lists
• Daily Outcomes	• Ideas
• Weekly Outcomes	• Notes
• Queues	• Monthly Results
• Scripts	

Organize Your Action Lists

Organizing your action information frees up your mind and creates one place to look for your actions. Action information can include your Daily Outcomes, Weekly Outcomes, queues, and scripts.

- **Daily Outcomes.** This is your list of Daily Outcomes that you create every day as outlines in Step 3.
- **Weekly Outcomes.** This is your list of Weekly Outcomes that you create as outlined in Step 4.
- **Queues.** For thing you can't accomplish in a single day, you need a place to store your actions and ideas. Make a list for each activity, project or chunk of work that you're focused on. This is where you put actions and outcomes that you aren't working on today but need to remember. It's where you store state without cluttering your head. Keeping organized lists, whether on paper or electronically, helps you organize your thinking while letting your mind work on more important things other than task lists. Your

queues are inputs into your Daily Outcomes and Weekly Outcomes.
- **Scripts.** A script is simply a written set of steps to perform a particular task. Scripts can help with complex activities or when you are trying to build a new habit. It's easier to follow a script than to have to spend a lot of energy thinking your way through a task each time.

Organize Your Reference Lists

Organizing your reference information frees up your mind and creates one place to look for your reference information: a repository for any notes you might need and a dumping ground for your ideas.
- **Ideas.** This is your personal depot of ideas. These could turn into actions, but while they are ideas, they are simply a reference list of interesting thoughts or ideas.
- **Notes.** This is your personal knowledge base. It's all the little tidbits of information and notes you collect. Consolidate these and don't mix them in with your action information.
- **Monthly Results.** At the end of each month, make a simple list of your most important results you accomplished. This helps remind you of what you got done and helps you build momentum.

Keep the following points in mind:
- This is a baseline system to help you get started. Adjust it as you see fit.
- The most important thing is that you consolidate and factor out your action items from your reference information.
- The next most important thing is that you have one place to look for your information, whether you use pen and paper, a simple file system of text files, or some personal information management software.

Adopting Monthly Improvement Sprints

Think of these as monthly improvement sprints. Pick one thing to improve, learn, or try out for the month. Each month, pick something new. This gives you a chance to cycle through 12 things over the year. You can always repeat a sprint. The idea is that a month is enough time to experiment with your results. You might not see progress after the first couple of weeks while you're learning, but a month is a good chunk of time to check your progress. In fact, your first Monthly Improvement Sprint can be adopting Agile Results; test-drive it for a month. Take your lessons learned from the month, carry the good forward, and use it to refine your approach.

Adopting Additional Practices

You can adopt additional practices as you see fit by drawing from the practices below:

Category	Practices
Rhythm of Results	• Daily, Weekly, Monthly Results
Mindsets and Motivation	• Compelling "Why" • Switch Hats
Time	• Allocated Time • Boundaries • Buffers • Fix Time, Flex Scope
Energy	• Park It • Power Hours
Learning	• Improvement Scripts • Lessons Learned • Pair Up
Planning	• Diversify Your Results • Reduce Open Work • Tests for Success
Doing	• Batch and Focus • Chunk It Down • Do It, Review It, Improve It • Fail Fast • Good Enough for Now • Just Start • Scripts • Sweeping • Test Your Results
Organizing	• One Place to Look

Prioritizing	• MUST, SHOULD, COULD
	• Next Best Thing
	• Worst Things First

For a description of the practices, see "Cheat Sheet – Supporting Practices Defined."

How To – Have a Strong Week

Summary

This article shows you how to have a strong week. A strong week is one where you spend more time in your strengths and less time in your weaknesses. This boosts both your energy and results. Not spending enough time in your strengths will gradually drain you. Spending more time in your strengths renews you, rebuilds your energy, and unleashes your best results.

Contents

- Objectives
- Summary of Steps
- Step 1—Map Out Your Weaknesses
- Step 2—Map Out Your Strengths
- Step 3—Design a Strong Week

Objectives

- Learn a simple technique for spending more time in your strengths each week.
- Learn how to eliminate or consolidate activities that make you weak.
- Learn how to add strengths to your week to improve your energy and results.

Overview

Spending time in your weaknesses drains you. Whether it's people or tasks, the effect is the same. Spending time in your strengths is just the opposite. The more time you spend in your strengths, the more you renew and recharge your energy. In addition, spending time in your strengths improves your performance and gets better results. Think about it—you're spending more time doing what you're great at.

Unplanned and reactive, your weekly schedule can become a mess. Worse, you might structure your week in a way that reinforces spending considerable time in your weaknesses. The key is to be aware of your weaknesses and identify your strengths. With this knowledge, you can be deliberate about how you spend your time. You can push back where it makes sense. Consolidate your weaknesses; rather than have them spread across your week and dominate your time, batch them together and limit the time spent on them. Furthermore, you can add more strengths to your week. Imagine getting your weaknesses out of the way, first thing, and then spending the rest of the day in your strengths? Restructuring your week and moving things around will dramatically improve your results.

When you do this exercise, don't be too concerned whether you can accurately tell weaknesses from strengths. You'll find it's a sliding scale. The key is to take the first step towards being aware. Once you start paying attention to what makes you weak or what makes you strong, use it to improve your daily and weekly results. You don't need to suddenly get rid of all your weaknesses or suddenly spend all your time in your strengths. It's an ongoing exercise where you incrementally spend more time in strengths and less time in weaknesses. By checking how you spend your time each week, you'll gradually shift. As you shift, you'll produce more effective results in shorter periods of time. You'll have more energy and you'll enjoy what you do. This is the essence of a strong week.

Summary of Steps
- Step 1—Map Out Your Weaknesses
- Step 2—Map Out Your Strengths
- Step 3—Design a Strong Week

Note: In the following steps, we'll focus on just Monday through Friday. You can include weekends too if you want, but I suggest first getting a handle on the core week days, before worrying about the weekend. The exception is if your work week starts on a Sunday, then I would start there.

Step 1—Map Out Your Weaknesses

In this step, think of the activities you do during the week and identify the ones that make you weak. Trust your gut. You can use a whiteboard or a sheet of paper. Think of it like a heat map; scan your week quickly for your key activities and identify whether they drain you. If that doesn't work for you, then walk through each day and determine which activities make you weak. Chances are, when you first do this, it will look like a scatter chart. Your weak activities will scattered throughout the day.

Example of Mapping Out Your Weaknesses

Here is an example of a map of activities that are weaknesses throughout the week:

	Mon	Tue	Wed	Thu	Fri
7:00 a.m.					
8:00					
9:00	W		W		
10:00	W				W
11:00		W			
12:00		W		W	
1:00 p.m.	W				W
2:00					
3:00	W		W		W
4:00		W	W		
5:00					
6:00					
7:00					
8:00					
9:00					
10:00					

Rather than use a "W," you can identify the actual activity that makes you weak. What's important is that you can easily see how the weaknesses are spread out.

Checkpoint

- *Can you identify the top three activities that make you the weakest?*
- *Can you identify the types of work that make you weak?*
- *Can you identify who drains you and who catalyzes you? What's the pattern?*

Step 2—Map Out Your Strengths

In this step, think of the activities you do during the week and identify the ones that make you strong. These are the activities that come easy for you and you enjoy doing. At first, your strong activities are probably like a scatter chart, just like your weaknesses. Awareness is the first step.

Example of Mapping Out Your Strengths

Here is an example of activities that are strengths throughout the week:

	Mon	Tue	Wed	Thu	Fri
7:00 a.m.					
8:00					
9:00		S		S	S
10:00		S			
11:00					
12:00	S		S		
1:00 p.m.					
2:00					S
3:00					
4:00					
5:00					
6:00					
7:00					
8:00					
9:00					
10:00					

Rather than use an "S," you can identify the actual activity that makes you strong. What's important is that you can easily see how the strengths are spread out.

Checkpoint

- *Can you identify the top three activities that make you strong?*
- *Can you identify the types of work that make you strong?*
- *Can you identify the patterns of people that catalyze you?*

Step 3—Design a Strong Week

In this step, you design a strong week. You do this by eliminating weaknesses, adding strengths, and consolidating any weaknesses that remain.

Eliminate Your Weaknesses

If there are activities that make you weak that you can get rid of, do so. This makes more room for your strengths. For many of people, this means eliminating some meetings, renegotiating some current tasks, or delegating them out.

Consolidate Your Weaknesses

Consolidate weaknesses that you can't get rid of. Adopt a "worst things first" practice by getting your weaknesses out of the way each morning. This creates a glide path for the rest of the day, especially as you add more strengths.

Add Strengths

Add activities that make you strong. This may require negotiation with your team, your manager, or your family, but in the long run, everyone benefits from your renewed vigor for life as you get more from your day to day. You might find that it's tough to add activities that make you strong. Start simple and don't rush. For example, you might schedule a weekly lunch with a mentor or friend that lifts you up; or perhaps, scheduling time with yourself—some quiet, alone time—is what recharges you. You also might find some simple ways to adjust the work you are already doing to play to your strengths. Get creative. The more focus and energy you put on playing to your strengths, the more you'll amplify your results. While you might get some quick wins under your belt, it's really a winning strategy for the long run. Continue improving your weekly schedule over time by adding more strengths and eliminating more weaknesses.

Example of a Strong Week

Here is an example of a strong week by design:

	Mon	Tue	Wed	Thu	Fri
7:00 a.m.					
8:00					
9:00	W	W	W	W	W
10:00	S	S	S	S	S
11:00					
12:00		S		S	
1:00 p.m.	S				
2:00			S		
3:00		S		S	
4:00	S		S		S
5:00					
6:00					
7:00					
8:00					
9:00					
10:00					

Notice that weaknesses are consolidated, and there are strengths throughout the week and throughout each day. In fact, one key way to improve your energy later in the day is to add activities that make you strong.

Guidelines

- Consolidate your weaknesses as best as you can. For example, you might use the first hour of each of your day as a timebox for activities that make you weak.
- Add more activities that make you strong.
- Start with something simple. You don't need to make it all or nothing. Simple wins add up. Eliminating even a few weaknesses really lifts a weight from your shoulders. Likewise, adding a few strengths renews your energy and makes thing happen.
- Pair up with people. You might find that pairing up on things that make you weak helps you enjoy them more. You might also find that you get more from your strengths when you pair up or team up with others.
- Test your results. Rather than try to predict results, test combinations and observe what happens. Pay attention to how you feel. Simply making a few shifts in your weekly schedule can dramatically impact your energy.

Checkpoint

- *Have you eliminated as many of the activities that make you weak as you can?*
- *Have you found a way to add a few activities that make you stronger?*
- *Have you consolidated your weaknesses as best as you can?*

Additional Resources for
Getting Results the Agile Way

Thank you for reading this guide. I hope that you're well on your way to getting the meaningful results that you're looking for.

To refer to this book online and for additional news, tools, and resources (such as cheat sheets, templates, how-tos, videos, and other supplementary information), please visit this book's Website: http://GettingResults.com